D1288249

INDEPENDENCE, MISSOURI

INDEPENDENCE, MISSOURI

BERND FOERSTER

THE HERITAGE COMMISSION

JAMES A. RYAN
MELVIN A. SOLOMON
ROBERT J. CLAYBAUGH
ERIC FOWLER

Copyright © 1978 Independence Press

Printed in the United States of America by *Independence Press,* 1978.

Library of Congress Cataloging in Publication Data
Foerster, Bernd.
Independence, Missouri

Includes index.
1. Historic sites—Missouri—Independence.
2. Independence, Mo.—Buildings. I. Title.
F474.13F63   977.8'41   78-2287
ISBN 0-8309-0203-1

This project was financed in part through a comprehensive grant from the Department of Housing and Urban Development under the provision of Section 701 of the Housing Act of 1954, as amended.

Table of Contents

Acknowledgments

The survey on which this book is based was financed in part by a grant from the Department of Housing and Urban Development and funding by the City of Independence, Missouri. It was approved and encouraged by Mayor Richard A. King; City Council members E. Lee Comer, Jr., Charles E. Cornell, Ray A. Heady, Dr. Duane Holder, Mitzi A. Overman, and Dr. Ray Williamson; former City Council members Arthur W. Lamb, Sam LeVota, and Morris McQuinn; and former City Manager Lyle Alberg. The grant was administered by the Planning Department, whose director, William Bullard; staff member, Paul Mosiman; and archives technician, W. Patrick O'Brien, facilitated the project.

The survey was conducted for the Heritage Commission of the City of Independence with the continuous assistance of its members: Bishop G. Leslie DeLapp, Robert S. Everitt, Pauline Fowler, Hazel Graham, Charles Kerr, the Reverend Thomas G. Melton, and Dr. Benedict K. Zobrist; and new members Florence Carson and Max Kaplan.

The following individuals deserve special thanks:

Bernd Foerster, professor and Dean of the College of Architecture and Design at Kansas State University, Manhattan, who, in addition to his role in the organization and supervision of the survey and the evaluation of its results, conceived the arrangement of the book, designed its layout, did the preliminary rewriting and editing of the historical material, contributed to the introduction, and wrote the chapter on future directions.

James A. Ryan, historian, employed by Solomon and Claybaugh, who performed the major portion of the research for the project, wrote the preliminary draft of the historical material, and served as project administrator for the consultants.

6

Melvin A. Solomon and Robert J. Claybaugh, architects, whose firm contracted with the City of Independence to conduct the survey upon which this book is based and who served as consultants for the entire project.

Eric Fowler, who, at the request of the Heritage Commission, performed additional research, writing, and editing for this book and assisted the editing committee of the commission: Pauline Fowler, chairman; Robert S. Everitt; and Benedict K. Zobrist.

Pauline Fowler, whose knowledge of local history and sources substantially contributed to the development of the historical information contained in this book and who helped guide the project from its inception, beginning with her own early historical survey through the preliminary drafts to the final editing and publication of the text.

Robert S. Everitt, who effectively served as liaison between the consultants and the Heritage Commission and who provided useful solutions to editorial considerations of the final text.

Benedict K. Zobrist, who provided leadership for the Heritage Commission, wrote portions of the Introduction, gave helpful criticism of the early drafts, and contributed historical information and editorial suggestions during the final editing.

Verne Christensen, who prepared the maps; Enell Foerster, who typed many copies of the early drafts; Jay Johnson, who assisted with the graphic design for the book.

The photographs, other than those obtained from sources listed below, were taken by Michael Schuetz, Jay Johnson, Melvin A. Solomon, and Bernd Foerster: Raymond E. Blake, page 77; William J. Curtis, page 2; the City of Independence, page 126; the B. F. Thomson Papers, Jackson County Historical Archives, page 40; Max Kaplan, page 2; *St. Louis Post Dispatch,* page 219; Milo E. Tinkham, page 148.

The following agencies, organizations, and companies provided important information: Chicago Title Insurance Company; Jackson County Historical Society Archives; Jackson County Probate Court; Jackson County Recorder of Deeds Office; Kansas City Museum of History and Science; Missouri Valley Room of the Kansas City, Missouri, Public Library; Missouri Water Company; and the Truman Library and Museum.

The following individuals were helpful during the research phase of the project: Gordon Apperson, Marie Blackburn; David Boutros, Col. Rufus Burrus, Glenn R. Colliver; Elizabeth Costin, William J. Curtis, David Ellender, Nancy M. Ehrlich, Alberta Franciskato, Martha Hatfield, Jack Henry, Susie Hinson, Marjorie Kinney, Vicki McClendon, Beth Pessek, Peggy Smith, Abby Taylor, Harold Whitehead, Delores Wilson, Pearl Wilcox, and Virginia Wright.

And an extra special thanks to the many unnamed citizens who graciously answered the requests for information, delved into family mementoes to provide clues and proof of accuracy in the historical sections. Without their help many interesting details would have been missed.

Introduction

Many of us don't really know or remember the Independence we live in—only certain tracks: house to work, house to school, house to store, house to house. Entire sections of our city are foreign or forgotten territory; even along the paths we frequently take, we have stopped seeing.

Neither do others really see the Independence they visit. Without a guide, they are unlikely to recognize much of the city's original character and historic development. Important occurrences have left some remains, but traces of a frenetic 1840s frontier town or a gracious 1890s arbored county seat conflict with first impressions today. Entrance to the city on Noland Road is along a strip that could exist anywhere in the United States. Fortunately for both residents and visitors, however, there are significant governmental and private efforts now underway to combat this civic amnesia and neglect.

The present high degree of interest and concern for the preservation of our historic heritage dates from February 1972 when the United States Department of the Interior surveyed and added the Harry S. Truman Historic District to the list of National Historic Landmarks associated with the lives of the Presidents of the United States. When Secretary of the Interior Stewart L. Udall first broached the subject in 1964, President Truman responded characteristically: "I must say to you, that in the past I have been reluctant to contribute to any effort designed to commemorate my Presidency. But the scope of your plan is such that I must now think about it. Perhaps we can go into it some time when I am in Washington."

The matter was not reopened until the summer of 1971 when officials of the National Park Service and the Truman Library again reviewed the subject. The spirit of the moment was caught by Dr. Ernest A. Connally, a Park Service historian: "Reflecting on the way home, I felt a sense of elation that our discussions in Independence were the first steps in an important development." In the fall of that year, the Trumans indicated they had no objections to such action and asked only that there be no ceremony marking the event.

A team of Park Service historians carefully surveyed the North Delaware Street neighborhood which reflects the life and career of President Truman. As a boy, he lived nearby, and after their marriage in 1919 he and Bess Wallace Truman resided at the famous 219 North Delaware address. Of particular interest to the historians, however, was the exceptional quality of what they found in Independence: Within only a few blocks of the Trumans' home were located the Presidential Library and Museum, the churches where Bess and Harry attended Sunday school and were married, the Jackson County Courthouse where Mr. Truman served as county judge, many other Truman-related landmarks, and much of the rich frontier history of Independence.

Both the city officials of Independence and neighbors of the Trumans were delighted with the national attention being given to Independence. Warned by the Department of the Interior of the continuing need to maintain those qualities of national significance for which the historic property received its federal recognition, citizen groups immediately began working with the City of Independence to develop proper legislation which would protect the integrity of the Landmark district.

Under the leadership of Mayor Phil K. Weeks, in May 1973 the City Council of Independence created a Heritage Commission consisting of seven members. By ordinance, the Commission is entrusted with encouraging preservation and enhancement of the historic and aesthetic values of the Truman neighborhood and any other sites which the Commission may recommend that the City Council establish as heritage districts. Among its early accomplishments, the Heritage Commission prepared and the City Council passed an ordinance establishing architectural and landscaping standards within the Truman Heritage District.

In 1974 the Commission realized that a comprehensive architectural and historical survey of the entire city was needed in order to assess the community's total heritage. With this in mind, in 1975 the Commission engaged an architectural firm to seek out the remaining elements of historic and favorable environmental value in Independence and to prepare this book. Some four hundred buildings and sites were initially identified and are listed beginning on page 230. From this initial list the Commission selected more than one hundred structures and sites for further study and presentation in this book.

The examples included here are typical of a historical period or architectural style rather than all-inclusive and represent a wide range of different socioeconomic levels. The absence of any particular structure or site from this book is no indication that its destruction might not constitute an intolerable loss. The members of the Heritage Commission also recognize that there are no absolute standards for judging the importance of historic environments. However, as in other fields, extensive exposure, observation, analysis, and enjoyment improve one's capacity to recognize quality.

By exercising this capacity, it is easily seen that Independence has a rich history. Much physical evidence from her fascinating past survives. In addition to the Truman neighborhood, other neighborhoods have retained qualities of an earlier day that could be enhanced to the benefit of the entire community. To deprive the city of the quality of these neighborhoods and to erase what can give insight into life at another time would impoverish our lives as well as those of future generations.

Nevertheless, mere inclusion on a list or in a book or a heritage district gives no assurance of proper maintenance, nor does it give a guarantee against destruction. These are provided for by the continued understanding and active interest of an involved citizenry. This book is intended to further arouse that understanding and interest.

This book is also the first step in implementing a broad historic preservation program. As a souvenir of Independence, it touches on the city's major historical developments and illustrates a few of the treasures which still exist. As a guide to Independence, it helps us know and see the Independence we live in and visit. As a catalog of Independence, this book is intended to provide the incentive to encourage even more historic preservation.

THE HERITAGE COMMISSION

12

Early Years

By act of the General Assembly of Missouri organizing Jackson County on December 15, 1826, three commissioners were appointed to select a location for the seat of justice, known from its creation as Independence. These three commissioners chose a 160-acre tract dominated by a heavily wooded ridge with several springs three miles south of the Missouri River. On March 29, 1827, the Circuit Court met at the home of John Young near the Big Blue River to confirm the commissioners' site selection. After the new county court also approved the site, the first sale of town lots occurred on July 9 through 11 of that year.

Independence immediately became the marketing center for the surrounding agricultural area, settled primarily by immigrants from Kentucky and Virginia. Its geographic location was favorable for the developing trade with Mexico. Land transportation from St. Louis did not have to cross the Missouri River before or after passing through Independence on the way toward the southwest. The town was also close enough to the Missouri River to have supplies from boats brought in for transfer to wagon trains. As early as 1827 Independence had begun to be used as the starting point for the Santa Fe Trail.

Travelers and visitors to Independence were quick to notice the town's prosperity and probable future importance. Charles Latrobe, a traveling companion of Washington Irving, wrote in 1832:

The town of Independence was full of promise, like most of the innumerable towns springing up in the midst of the forests of the West, many of which, though dignified by high-sounding epithets, consist of nothing but a ragged congeries of five or six rough log huts, two or three clapboard houses, alias grogshops; a few stores, a bank, printing office and barn-looking churches. It lacked at the time I commemorate, the last three edifices, but was nevertheless a thriving and aspiring place. . . .

A different group of visitors had arrived in Independence more than a year earlier. In the winter of 1830-31 five elders of the Church of Jesus Christ of Latter Day Saints were sent to western Missouri to convert the Indians living immediately to the west. In line with their instructions to come here, some of these missionaries settled in Independence to support the work of the group and send reports about this new country to church headquarters in Kirtland, Ohio.

Joseph Smith, Jr., prophet and founder of the church, visited Independence in July and August of 1831 and revealed that this would be the center place for Zion. The church members, commonly known then as Mormons, raised funds to purchase land in and around Independence and to finance the migration of other members to the area to establish Zion.

Independence was only four years old and lacked many amenities, but the incoming Mormons—primarily from New York and Ohio—worked industriously to realize their goal of an earthly paradise. They built homes, started a school, operated a ferry, farmed, opened stores and churches, and published two newspapers, one directed toward members and the other toward secular society. The Mormons also brought with them a deep-seated evangelistic belief in their religious and social philosophy. However, some were overzealous in their attempts to share the good news with their new neighbors, to claim this land as their inheritance, and to expostulate against the evils of slavery. This gave birth to a feeling among some of the older settlers that both Independence and Jackson County would be far better off without the Mormons. Whatever the mixture of reasons—such as religious intolerance and fear of loss of political and economic control—motivating each individual who took part, a strong movement developed to expel the Mormons. They were driven out of Jackson County in November 1833, only six years after the site of Independence was established.

At the time of its founding, Independence was the westernmost settlement in the United States; it was also near the Missouri River, astride old Indian and hunter trails, and close to Indian territory. It was in the best location to benefit from the 1825 United States treaties with the Osage and Kansa Indians, the Indian Removal Act of 1830, the Santa Fe trade, and the westward migrations of the eighteen forties and fifties.

The 1825 treaties opened Jackson County land for private ownership and settlement. The Indian Removal Act caused almost all Indians to be moved from their lands within the limits of the United States east of the Mississippi to the great American desert west of Missouri. The Indians were paid annuities for their confiscated land and many of the pioneers of Jackson County thrived on the sale of flour, corn, cloth, blankets, pots and pans, guns, and illegal whiskey to the displaced redmen settled only a few miles away.

In 1821 the Santa Fe Trail began farther east in Franklin, Missouri, but to reduce the overland distance to Mexico, caravans began to be loaded first at Fort Osage and then in Independence. By 1832 Independence had become the outfitting headquarters for mule- and ox-drawn wagon trains. Reports of enormous profits by returning traders soon led to the development of wagons capable of carrying up to seven thousand pounds of merchandise.

Supplies poured in from the east. Samuel Owens, a Santa Fe merchant and freighter from Independence, ordered the following items in 1840: Jersey prints, Irish linen, tobacco, children's gloves, indigo, thread, blankets, and gray cashmere. Other articles sent to Santa Fe in the eighteen forties included coffee, flour, loaf sugar, candlewicks, shoe blacking, fine china, tumblers, and a few books.

Independence and the county also increased. Early county records mention frequent construction and repair of roads and bridges for the convenience of travelers, traders, and residents as well as the licensing of numerous taverns and ferries. Federal records show that many of the early licenses allowing trade with the Indians to the west were granted to Independence merchants and craftsmen. Several of these men were also early county officials who were engaged in some aspect of Santa Fe and immigrant commerce.

The city, because of its prior experience and success in servicing the Santa Fe trade, was equipped to become a major outfitting base for the westward migration. By 1848 it was estimated that there were more than twelve thousand people in Oregon—most of whom had begun their trek in Independence. Many of the California gold prospectors of 1849 also were funneled through Independence.

Independence was thus gaining enough in importance and population so that it was no longer necessary for it to be administered by the county court. On March 8, 1849, the Missouri General Assembly granted Independence a home-rule charter. The first vote by the citizens of Independence to accept the charter failed. The second vote, on June 23, 1849, passed and on July 18, 1849, William McCoy, merchant, banker and Santa Fe trader, was elected the first mayor.

It was during the late eighteen forties, however, that the town of West Port—Independence was the east port of entry—ended the virtual monopoly Independence had held in outfitting traders and migrants. West Port, as its name implies, was farther west, with more good pastureland immediately available. Its location made it unnecessary for the wagon trains to cross the Big Blue River in Jackson County, perhaps the most difficult crossing on the trails west at that time. To compete with these advantages, Independence merchants financed the construction of what is now called the first railroad west of the Mississippi. Cars were pulled by mules and the tracks extended from Wayne City Landing on the Missouri River to the Square. The railroad brought supplies from riverboats to the city, where they could be transferred to wagons. Unfortunately, the railroad was abandoned in 1852 because of financial problems.

In retrospect, the greatest problem to the continued growth of Independence may have been slavery. Missouri had been admitted to the Union as a slaveholding state in 1821. With the passage of the Kansas-Nebraska Act of 1854, which allowed the citizens of Kansas Territory to decide whether they would be admitted to the Union as residents of a slave or free state, a bloody feud began on the western border of Jackson County and Missouri. This border war which erupted in 1855 and served as a prelude to the Civil War, brought a rapid decline in the Independence outfitting trade.

Culturally, Independence was a southern town. During the eighteen thirties, forties, and fifties, as the area's population increased and its citizens became wealthier, the number of slaves in Jackson County increased from 193 in 1830 to 3,944 in 1860. In 1861 a group of citizens raised a Confederate flag over the city, but Secessionist and Union sympathies were divided. Kansas Jayhawkers and Quantrill's southern guerrillas met in skirmishes and pillaged the county. Unnecessary brutality was practiced by both sides, but it was Union depredations, especially Order No. 11, that evenually put most residents in the Secessionist camp.

Order No. 11, issued by Brigadier General Thomas A. Ewing on August 25, 1863, directed all inhabitants of Jackson, Cass, and Bates counties and part of Vernon County to leave their homes within 15 days. Those who took an oath of allegiance to the Union were to move to a Federal post. All others were banished from the district. The abandoned homes and outbuildings were then set afire in order to prevent sympathizers to the southern cause from giving aid to the guerrillas. When it finally became possible for the citizens to return to their homes, they found only their chimneys remaining. The area around Independence was so devastated that for years it was referred to as "the Burnt District."

Independence became a Federal post on June 7, 1862. On August 11 of that year, in the first Battle of Independence, Confederate troops fought their way southwest through the business district, causing some Union forces to surrender and others to escape to Kansas City, a Union stronghold. In late October 1864 the second Battle of Independence took place, and fighting occurred back and forth across the city for two days.

After the tragedies of the Civil War, Independence never recovered the prosperity in manufacturing and merchandising that it had enjoyed before, although some residents amassed large fortunes as a result of conditions spawned by the war, including the foreclosure of property of citizens who had fled.

For years the town suffered from divisiveness caused by the physical and emotional wounds experienced by many residents during the Civil War. The more cohesive citizenry of neighboring Kansas City was able to secure the railroads and thus assume economic and political leadership in the county. The citizens of Independence became more introverted and began to focus on their family, social, and religious ties.

From its inception, and even throughout its rip-roaring trail days, many residents of Independence adhered to their religious faiths. Before churches were formally organized, the members of most denominations were served by itinerant preachers. A Baptist church was built beside the road from Fort Osage to Independence in 1825. A Presbyterian congregation was founded in 1826 in a house three miles southwest of where Independence was to be located the next year, and a Presbyterian church was constructed in town in 1837. The Methodist church was established in 1835, the Christian church in 1836. Roman Catholics in the community were served by traveling priests until a parish was organized in 1845. By the start of the Civil War, all major Christian denominations in the United States were represented in the city. The Second Baptist church, one of the foremost institutions in the black community, was organized in 1861. St. Paul African Methodist Episcopal (A.M.E.) church was founded in 1866.

Hiram Young, a charter member of the A. M. E. church, is the best known of the early blacks. One of the finest blacksmiths and wagonmakers in the city, he bought his freedom from slavery and by 1860 owned real estate worth $36,000 and personal property worth $20,000. Young fled Independence during the war. He later returned and rebuilt his woodworking business. The first public school for blacks in Independence was renamed in his honor.

Although there were a few small private schools during the city's early years, the Independence public school system was not organized until 1866. The Independence Female College was founded in 1869, as was coeducational Woodland College. Saint Mary's Academy was organized by the Roman Catholic Church in 1878.

Independence was now more than 40 years old. Fortunately, in that brief period, the enmities engendered by the Civil War and the intellectual and emotional insularity dating back as far as the persecution of the Latter Day Saints were not reflected in the physical appearance of the town. In 1871 a special correspondent of the St. Louis *Republican* visited Independence. His observations appeared in the Independence *Sentinel,* June 24, 1871:

This is what might be termed an orchard town beautifully located, and where the dwelling houses are so hidden by foliage and large clumps of forest trees which have been left standing, that one could scarcely believe at a glance down the green avenues that the place was inhabited; but when in my rambles I discovered the homes, how prettily they looked with their neat porches covered with roses and honey suckle and all manner of sweet climbing shrubs and flowers; there was presented to my view sweet homes nestled in the trees, where no storm could apparently ever reach, but at all times would be blessed with a smooth current of domestic joy and happiness.

FLOURNOY HOUSE
1233 West Lexington

ca. 1826

Jones H. Flournoy, merchant and Indian trader, lived in this house in the eighteen twenties and thirties when it stood at 126 South Pleasant. He and Joseph Smith, Jr., might have met here in August 1831 to discuss the purchase of some land west of his house. On December 19, 1831, Flournoy sold the 63.43-acre tract now known as the Temple Lot for $130 to the 20-month-old Latter Day Saints Church.

In 1963 Flournoy's former residence was saved from demolition and moved to 1107 South Cottage by William J. Curtis. The building was later moved to its present location on the Temple Lot, restored and converted to a museum.

LOG COURTHOUSE
107 West Kansas

1827

Builder: Daniel P. Lewis, Independence, Missouri

This temporary courthouse was constructed for Jackson County by Daniel P. Lewis at a cost of $150. It is the oldest county courthouse still in existence west of the Mississippi River. Sam Shepherd, a black slave, reputedly hewed the oak logs. The county court held its first meeting here on August 11, 1828.

In 1916 the building was given to Independence by Mayor Christian Ott and moved to its current site from its original location at the southeast corner of Lexington and Lynn. Its present restoration dates from the early nineteen twenties and was supervised by William Stewart McCoy. In 1932 and 1933 Judge Harry S. Truman demonstrated his appreciation of historic structures by holding county court meetings here while the courthouse on the Square was being enlarged and remodeled.

HENLEY - WILLIAMSON RESIDENCE
3940 South Crysler

ca. 1830

One former owner of this farmhouse, Alonzo F. Henley, was president of an Independence bank and owner of 12 slaves. He died in 1861, leaving the house to his wife. Because of their great wealth and sympathies with the Southern cause, the family was harassed by border raiders before fleeing to Kentucky until after the war. Since 1891 the house has been in the Williamson family.

NOLAND - WHITE RESIDENCE
1024 South Forest

ca.1850

This two-story front section was built for Smallwood Noland, innkeeper, who came from Kentucky and bought the property in 1833. The two-room rear section probably dates from 1831. Noland took a prominent part in the persecution and expulsion of the Latter Day Saints in 1833. He was listed in the 1840 census as the owner of 10 slaves. By 1850 he was worth $30,000 and owned 26 slaves.

Since 1899 the house has been the property of the Jason White, Sr., family. The surrounding fields contribute substantially to the authenticity of the setting.

WOODLAWN CEMETERY
701 South Noland Road

ca. 1837

This final resting place of Independence pioneers once may have been an Indian burial ground. The first white owner was Robert Rickman, who patented the land in 1833. The land was already in use as a cemetery prior to 1845, the year it became an official county burial ground. The cemetery includes graves of early settlers, traders and merchants from the days of the Santa Fe trail, Civil War soldiers, a former slave who bought his freedom, a black man who was a messenger for Quantrill's raiders, and a sheriff murdered by outlaws.

KRITSER RESIDENCE
115 East Walnut

1847

Martin L. Kritser, an early-day Independence grocer originally from Virginia, had this elegant cottage built with profits from an 1846 Santa Fe trading venture. A later owner, Patrick McCarty, was a bartender in a saloon on the Square. His wife held off railroad men with a shotgun until her husband could return to negotiate the sale of part of their property for the railroad right-of-way.

SPRING HOUSE
1300 East U.S. 24 Highway

ca. 1850

Located over a natural spring, the walls are built into a slope and protrude only about halfway above the ground. The doorway is turned away from the sun and opens into a sluice that runs into a pond. The construction material of the spring house walls and sluice is of squared limestone and limestone rubble. Before the advent of mechanical refrigeration, this type of structure was commonplace.

OVERFELT - JOHNSTON RESIDENCE
305 South Pleasant

ca. 1850

Virginian John A. Overfelt, the original owner of this residence, came to Independence from St. Louis. Overfelt, who operated a successful steam-powered mill, served on the city council for many years. He was elected for the last time in 1870.

In 1860 the house was foreclosed by William Chrisman. It was bought by Granville Page, a slave dealer, on the courthouse steps. Later it was sold for back taxes to Mary Ellis. After the war, she sold the house back to Granville Page for the amount it had cost her.

In 1867 the house was purchased by Courtney Campbell and has since remained in his family. Today, the house is occupied by Campbell's granddaughter, Harriett Campbell Johnston, "Miss Cammie," who was born in the house.

CEMETERY
Opposite 921 Dickinson Road

ca. 1850

In 1882 John T. Smith, wealthy gentleman farmer, sold 40 acres, including this site, to Hartwell Tucker, a black farmer. Two years later Tucker wrote in his will: "Grave yard to be retained for family use." The cemetery has been in use until recent years.

LEWIS - WEBB RESIDENCE
302 West Mill

ca. 1853

The smaller one-story back section was built about 1834.
The front half was built about 1853 for John Lewis, a
pioneer saddler and community leader who came to
Independence from Madison County, Kentucky, in the mid
eighteen twenties. The property has changed ownership
numerous times, but is remembered as the Webb house
because historian William Larkin Webb lived here from
1902 until his death in 1931. The present Victorian facade
was adopted in the early eighteen eighties.

SUMMER KITCHEN
18525 R. D. Mize Road

ca. 1855

This summer kitchen, adjacent to the main house, was built for Samuel M. C. Saunders, farmer and slaveholder, who acquired the property in 1854. The stone for the structure was quarried south of the house. The property remained in the family until 1954.

The red brick house of John B. Saunders, brother of Samuel, located at 17601 R. D. Mize Road, is from the same period.

THOMSON RESIDENCE/RESTAURANT
9800 East U.S. 40 Highway

ca. 1855

The original owner was Benjamin Franklin Thomson, a Kentucky native who served in the Missouri General Assembly in 1850 and 1851. He also was elected to the prestigious office of sheriff of Jackson County for several terms. Thomson helped establish the First Christian Church in Independence, was a charter member of the local Royal Arch Masons and co-founder and president of the Jackson County Agricultural and Mechanical Association.

Bricks for this example of Greek Revival architecture were made on the site by slaves. When U.S. Highway 40 was built in 1935, the house was turned completely around to face the new highway. The building has served as a farmhouse, residence, and restaurant.

McCOY RESIDENCE
410 West Farmer

1856

The square front section of this house was built for William McCoy, who came to Independence from Ohio in 1838 and was elected the city's first mayor in 1849. He was a banker and Indian trader and lived here until his death in 1900.

The rectangular rear wing was built about 1840, probably for Samuel C. Owens, merchant and outfitter for the Santa Fe trade. The building has been restored by Mr. and Mrs. Forest Ingram.

MARSHAL'S HOUSE AND COUNTY JAIL/MUSEUM
217 North Main

1859

During the Civil War, the jail was used by the Union Army as a military prison; the marshal's house served as provost marshal's headquarters. Among the prisoners held in the jail were border war guerrilla leader William C. Quantrill, various Southern sympathizers, and Frank James. The jail also held nameless members of chain gangs who built roads in the Independence area until the nineteen thirties. After 1933 the structures were used as social service facilities. The marshal's house and jail have been preserved and restored by the Jackson County Historical Society and were officially opened as a museum and Society headquarters in 1959.

WOODSON RESIDENCE
1604 West Lexington

ca. 1866

   This country villa, erected for Samuel Hughes Woodson, lawyer and United States Congressman (1856-1861), was built in the then-popular Italianate style. Restoration work, begun in 1940 by Sidney Moore, was continued by Circuit Court Judge Marcus Kirtley when he acquired the property. In 1968 the house was purchased by Samuel Locke Sawyer, a descendant of the first owner.

WAGGONER - GATES MILL
526 South Osage

ca. 1875

A few imposing structures remain from this complex of buildings that housed the once vital Waggoner-Gates Milling Company, an important Independence industry since the mid-nineteenth century. John A. Overfelt operated a mill just north of the present site until 1866, when it was purchased by Peter Waggoner, father of William H. Waggoner. The two Waggoners continued the operation of Overfelt's mill until 1875, when the mill on the present site was started and the company was incorporated. Among those who incorporated the business were Judge E. P. Gates and George P. Gates. George P. Gates was the maternal grandfather of Bess Truman. The company manufactured Queen of the Pantry Flour, a product known nationwide.

Map of the Early Years

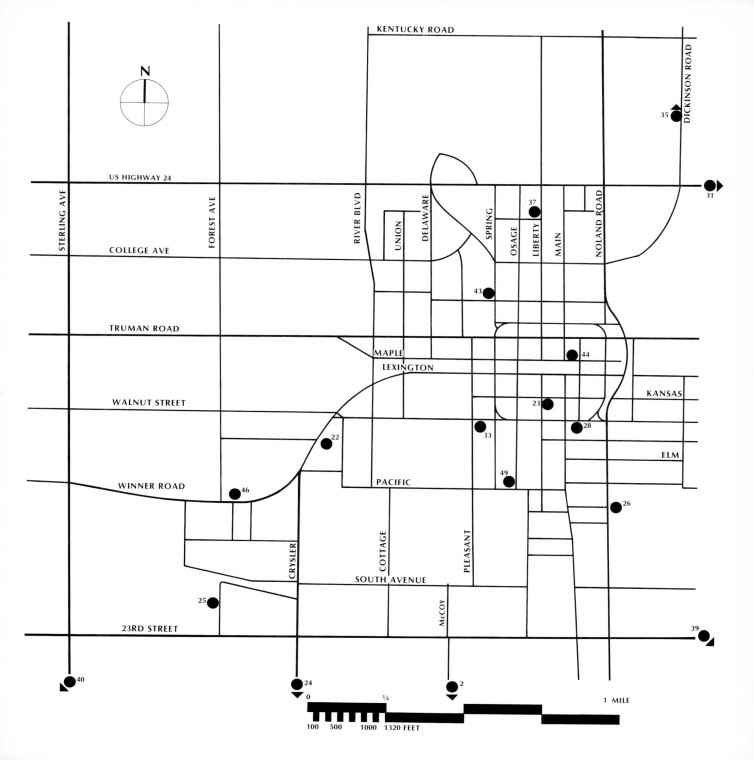

Boom Years

"Nature has formed and fashioned these grounds especially for the erection of elegant houses...," wrote an anonymous author about Independence in the early eighteen eighties. He described the area north of the city as a "most grand and beautiful country, being apparently set apart by the Creator, for the erection of magnificent residences, and the grounds for ornamentation. For a distance of over a mile...is one continuous orchard, embracing all the varieties of fruits known to the horticultural list susceptible of successful cultivation in this latitude."

These boastful comments foretold the immediate future of Independence. At the beginning of the decade

Independence was an ordinary county seat town with dirt streets, except about the public square, with a population of about thirty-five hundred, and no way to get to Kansas City except over a dirt road with almost impossible grades. A trip to Kansas City required a day. Between Independence and Kansas City . . .were about 30 houses. The Missouri Pacific Railroad operated a suburban train from the Liberty Street depot in Independence to the Second Street Station in Kansas City, and the fare was fifty-five cents for the round trip. The schedule of trains was uncertain.

All this was soon to change. A boulevard between Independence and Kansas City was opened in the fall of 1885 and in 1887 Willard E. Winner completed his Kansas City, Independence, and Park Railway for commuters and shoppers. Even though Winner eventually went bankrupt, it was his railway more than anything else which doubled and tripled land values and caused a building boom along present-day Independence Avenue, Highway 24, and Winner Road. The land on both sides of the boulevard and the railway was subdivided. Roads within the subdivisions made the building lots accessible to both Kansas City and Independence, first on the commuter line and later by trolley, bus, and automobile.

The Kansas City *Times* commented at the close of 1887:

A correct idea of the magnitude of the development and prosperity the city is now enjoying can be gained from the fact that the [real estate] transfers recorded during the year 1885 in sum total were but $1,022,000., in 1886 the grand aggregate of transfers was three times that of the previous year, or $3,102.000. During the year of 1887 the amount of transfers recorded was far beyond the expectation of the most sanguine, reaching $18,000,000., or six times that of the preceding year.

Even before prosperity returned, earlier hostile attitudes among the citizens toward outsiders were diminishing. In 1867 a few Latter Day Saints—members of what is now known as the Church of Christ-Temple Lot—returned to live in Independence. That same year the first Reorganized Latter Day Saint family purchased land north of Independence.

In the midst of this new prosperity, there were claims that Independence was "one of the finest residence cities in the land. Its citizens as a class are wealthy and many of Kansas City's prominent businessmen have handsome residences and grounds in the 'Royal Suburb.'"

Many of these handsome residences still survive, but the boom that produced them collapsed in 1888, with the value of land dropping nearly 70 percent in the next three years. Full recovery did not occur until after the turn of the century.

CHICAGO AND ALTON RAILROAD STATION
1411 West South Avenue

ca. 1880

Erected by the Chicago and Alton Railroad Company and later owned by the Gulf, Mobile and Ohio Railroad, this depot is now the property of the Illinois, Central and Gulf Railroad.

The two-story frame building has a variety of wood siding and is, except for boarded windows, notably blessed by lack of alterations.

RUMMEL RESIDENCE
147 East Lexington

ca. 1881

Almost unnoticed in its present surroundings, this building was built about 1855 for the Rummel family, German immigrants who came to Independence in the late eighteen forties. Rebuilt by local artisan Christian Yetter about 1881, its detailing resembles the home on 146 East Kansas, pictured on page 61.

POHLMEYER RESIDENCE
146 East Kansas

ca. 1881

Builder: Christian Yetter, Independence, Missouri

This well-preserved house was built by one of the best Independence craftsmen, Christian Yetter, for his brother-in-law, Henry Pohlmeyer, a baker.

Yetter is best remembered as the contractor for the 1910 city hall, the First Presbyterian Church, and over 150 county road bridges.

McCOY - DeWITT RESIDENCE
412 North Spring

1881

Samuel Locke Sawyer had this frame house built as a gift for his daughter, Fannie McCoy, wife of William L. McCoy, merchant, realtor, and nephew of the first mayor of Independence. The house is noteworthy for its porch with spindle frieze and turned posts with brackets.

DRUMM FARM SMOKEHOUSE
3210 Lee's Summit Road

1881

   This typical rolling Jackson County farmland was bought in 1912 by Major Andrew Drumm of Kansas City, Missouri, as a home for "parentless and friendless" boys. When he lived in Kansas City, Drumm was a livestock broker; he had previously been a California forty-niner and a Kansas rancher and banker. His will, read after his death in 1919, established an endowment for the continued operation of the boys' home. The smokehouse on the property is still used for curing ham and bacon.

VAILE MANSION
1500 North Liberty

1881

Architect: Asa Cross, Kansas City, Missouri
Brickmason: William M. Randall, Independence, Missouri

Designed in the Second Empire style, the Vaile mansion is celebrated for its complex slate roof, four-story tower, and elaborate porch across the east facade. Another noteworthy feature is the sheer abundance of nonrepetitive details applied to the exterior.

The first owner was Harvey Merrick Vaile, a native of Vermont and a man of wealth, whose enterprises included contract mail delivery for the United States. First a resident of Kansas City, Missouri, Vaile had this house built in 1881 and lived here until his death in 1895.

In 1908 the house became the Vaile Inn, a summer hotel, later a sanitarium, and finally a nursing home. The structure was accurately restored in 1974 by Waldemar Kurok, and Independence contractor, for Mrs. J. Roger DeWitt, the owner since 1960.

PORTER - CHILES RESIDENCE
522 West Maple

ca. 1883

Although originally constructed about 1860 for grocer David J. Porter, the building now illustrates the time of its remodeling, about 1883, when a front porch and center second-story gable patterned after the Vaile Mansion were added. The house was bought that year by Cornelius C. Chiles, a well-known citizen and banker who had come to Independence from Kentucky as a child in 1832 and eventually became superintendent of the Overland Mail. The house was the Maples Hotel for several years until it was recently returned to private ownership.

SECOND BAPTIST CHURCH
116 East White Oak

1886

This church was built by a black congregation founded in 1861 when one of its organizers, Lizzie Johnson, was still a slave. After the Emancipation Proclamation on January 1, 1863, church membership grew rapidly. In 1881 the congregation had 125 members.

The first meeting place the church owned was a frame building erected at 117 East Farmer in 1867. After the church moved to a larger building in the late 1870s, the East Farmer building was used as the first school for blacks in Independence. The first load of bricks used in construction of the 1886 church was donated by Emily Fisher, another founding member.

STAPLES RESIDENCE
526 South Liberty

ca. 1886

This one-story frame cottage is at once modest and complex, with intriguing combinations of forms, roof lines, and porch details.

Soon after the house was built, it became the property of William C. Staples, a pioneer farmer who retired here and became a beloved storyteller and local personality known as "Uncle Billy."

HUGHES-GREGG RESIDENCE
801 South Main

1887

Architects: Gibbs and Parker, Kansas City, Missouri
Builder: Christian Yetter, Independence, Missouri

Built for the sisters Mollie and Josie Hughes, this house typifies the gracious character of Independence residences of the nineteenth century. Designed in the Queen Anne style, this residence has splendid architectural configurations and details. A highly decorated porch wraps around the front wings and a unique circular tower containing a porch rises on the northwest corner of the second floor to an octagonal roof. The south facade contains an ornate two-story bay, hemispherical on the first story and rectangular above, and an elaborate cut-brick chimney.

Stanley Gregg, Independence banker and civic leader, acquired the residence in the 1930s. Since 1967 the house has been meticulously maintained in its original state by the present owners, Mr. and Mrs. "Petey" Childers.

BANK/COMMERCIAL BUILDING
200 North Liberty

ca. 1887

The first floor and parapet were modernized in 1915, but the old Bank of Independence building still retains some of the architectural character common to the Square before the turn of the century.

SOUTH SIDE OF THE SQUARE

ca. 1914

Some of these buildings on the south side of the Square date from the late 1800s and blend in nicely with today's buildings representing each decade of the 1900s. The whole Square area has the potential of becoming a completely integrated showcase of what historic restoration, preservation, and practical uses in conjunction with modern urban planning can accomplish.

BULLENE-CHOPLIN RESIDENCE
702 North Delaware

1887

The original owner was Thomas C. Bullene, a dry goods merchant on the Square. He was the eldest son of Thomas B. Bullene, a partner in the prestigious Kansas City dry goods firm of Bullene, Moore and Emery, later known as Emery, Bird, Thayer. Among the notable features of this house are the original second-story porch columns and brackets and the oriel tower with conical roof. The house has been renovated and preserved by Miss Josephine Choplin, whose family has owned the home since 1919.

SAWYER-JENNINGS RESIDENCE
510 North Delaware

ca. 1887

Builder: Thomas B. Smith, Independence, Missouri

Smith built this house for Aaron Flint Sawyer, an Independence banker. Sawyer family tradition indicates that the plans were first drawn by Stanford White of New York City; however, extant specifications for the house were handwritten and signed by Smith, not White.

Nearly the entire house is original, including the slate roof, the L-shaped porch with spindle frieze, and the three-story tower, a familiar landmark on Delaware Street. The tower has a circular first story and octagonal second and third stories supporting a pointed octagonal roof. The third story contains an open porch. Also noteworthy are a hall chandelier and a variety of stained-glass windows in the style of Louis C. Tiffany.

The present owners, Mr. and Mrs. Frank Jennings, have been honored by the Jackson County Historical Society for their preservation of the house.

FLETCHER-BOSTIAN RESIDENCE
602 North Delaware

1887

Builder: W. T. Cooper, Independence, Missouri

This residence was built for a widow, Mrs. Maria J. Fletcher, who took in boarders. The house was sold in 1905 to William Bostian, postmaster of Independence for 13 years. He was first appointed by President McKinley in 1901 and reappointed by Presidents Theodore Roosevelt and William H. Taft.

WILSON-COLYER RESIDENCE
602 East Lexington

ca. 1890

This residence was built for Samuel T. Wilson, son of John Wilson, one of the original founders of the Chrisman-Sawyer Banking Company. The house was also owned for several years by C. C. "Kit" Colyer, a major turn-of-the-century road builder in Jackson County.

The red brick house is distinguished by an octagonal tower at the southwest corner and porch gables set at forty-five-degree angles to the house.

WATSON-EBERLE RESIDENCE
720 West Maple

ca. 1888

This house was built for T. J. Watson, a retired physician who had served as a surgeon on General Grant's staff during the Civil War. The red brick residence contains fine terra-cotta ornament. It is also distinguished by its conical-roofed oriel tower, which extends from the second level to the attic, and by other ornate elements, including cut-brick chimneys. The house has been well preserved by its present owners Mr. and Mrs. John Eberle.

MIFFLIN RESIDENCE
108 South Overton

ca. 1889

The original owner was Samuel T. Mifflin; the house remained in the family until 1962. The ornamentation on the building is well preserved. Noteworthy are the fan-shaped decorations in the gables, the turned columns with elaborate brackets, and the band of fish-scale shingles between the floors.

Map of the Boom Years

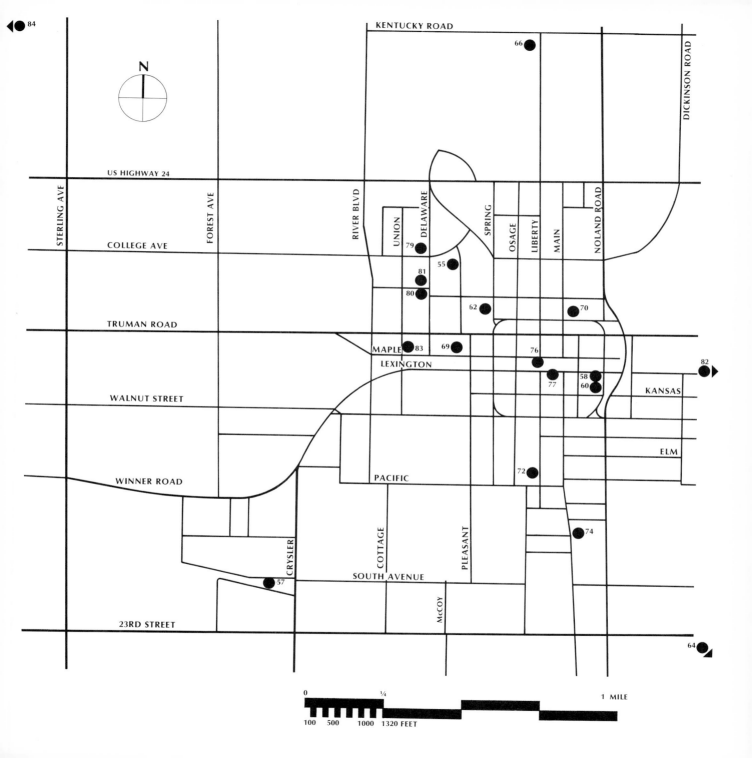

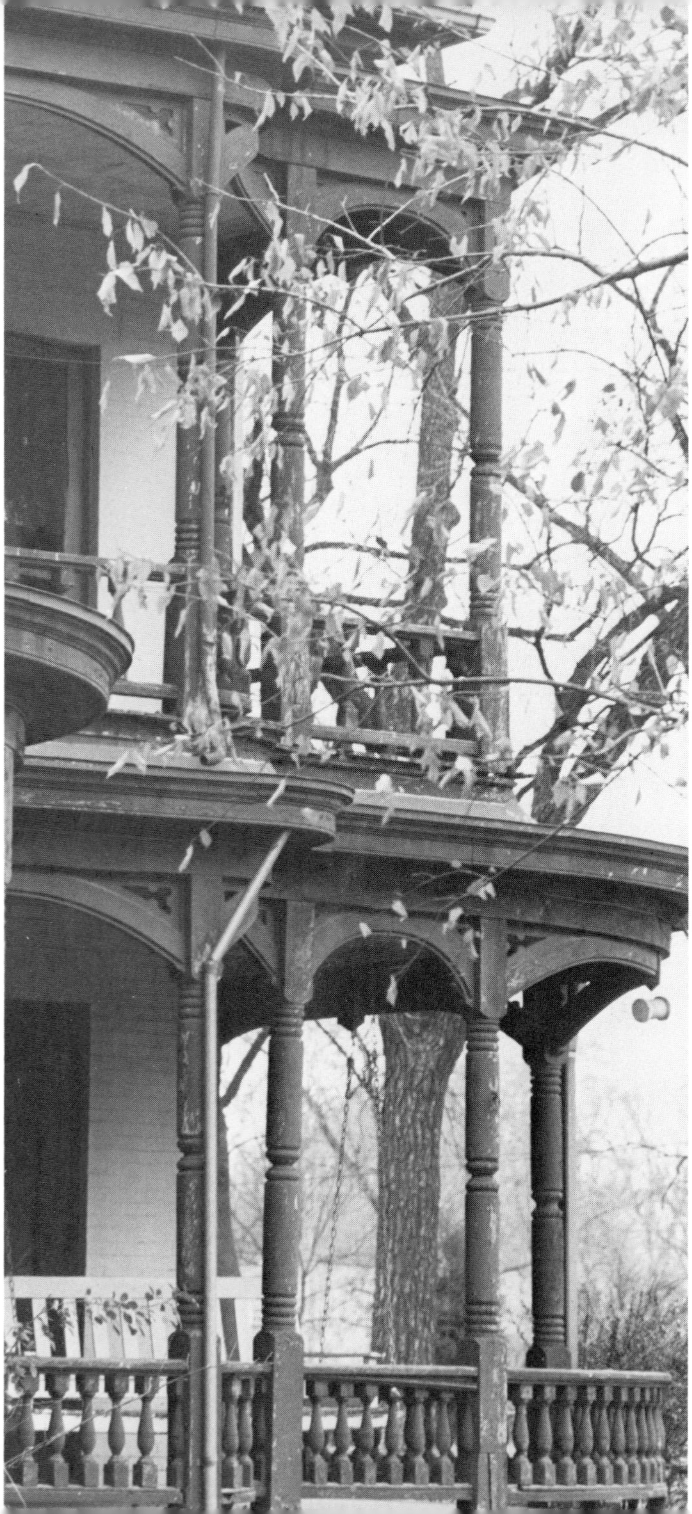

Growth Years

"'And what was all this country like?' I asked, pointing out the car window at the beautiful houses and well-kept lawns of South Main Street.

"'All wilderness,' he answered, 'wilderness.'"

So reminisced Levi Potts, a farmer, forty-niner, and Confederate soldier who had lived in Jackson and Johnson counties since 1829, to an Independence *Examiner* reporter in 1912.

By the turn of the century, the wilderness Potts remembered had been turned into rich farmland or gracious subdivisions and Independence had been transformed from a town into a prosperous agricultural center and county seat. Well-kept, commodious homes and attractive cottages and bungalows lined the tree-shaded streets. Family and social outings were held at Fairmount Park west of the city and at the county fairgrounds southeast of Fair Avenue and Noland Road. Church spires dominated the community scene. Recollections of the period describe an idyll of small town life.

From about 1906 to 1914, a burning question in Independence was the proposed annexation by Kansas City which was favored by some leading figures. It was a time of prosperity for both cities, but a growing civic spirit, led by William Southern, founder and editor of the *Examiner,* eventually assured that Independence would remain a separate community.

The quality of life must have been attractive because more and more new people were moving into the city. Between 1900 and 1910 the population of Independence increased from 6,974 to 9,859. Many of these new residents were Reorganized Latter Day Saint craftsmen and storekeepers moving to Zion. In 1908 an Independence woman commented, "I walked for a mile over an Independence street yesterday...and I never met a single person that I knew. I have lived in Independence for nearly 40 years and never realized that it would be possible to walk a block on a business street and not know everybody that I met. It must be that there are a great many new residents coming in all the time."

During this era, the front page of the Independence *Examiner* reflected the local citizens' interest and concern for their churches, clubs, societies, and each other. Weddings and deaths were front page news. News concerning the first local unit of the Parent-Teachers Association was reported. This organization was especially influential, succeeding in making Independence dry on January 1, 1915, several years before prohibition became a national policy. Meetings of the Daughters of the American Revolution and the United Daughters of the Confederacy were reported in detail. County and city politics were constantly in the news since Independence at this time was almost evenly divided between supporters of the Democratic and Republican parties. When national and international coverage was included, it was generally of the human interest variety.

All in all, Independence during this period was a typical American town whose residents were interested mostly in their own community. Elizabeth Paxton Forsling, a young Independence girl during the early 1900s, remembered that "band concerts were held on the Square. People would gather to listen and talk; girls and boys would walk around holding hands. The sparrows humming in the courthouse trees would compete with the band....It was...a lovely age of innocence."

BROOKSIDE FARM
16000 East Truman Road

1892

This excellent complex of farm buildings, including farm-house, barn, smokehouse, pump house, and several sheds, was built for Warren Watson, clerk of the United States Circuit Court, Kansas City, Missouri.

Beautifully sited on rolling terrain with rock out-croppings, the farm has been in the Bell family since 1900.

STEEPLE, ST. MARY'S ROMAN CATHOLIC CHURCH
611 North Liberty

1893

Construction of the church was begun in 1860. It was dedicated August 15, 1864.

The 110-foot octagonal steeple was designed by the Very Reverend Father Thomas J. Fitzgerald in 1893 and is an important visual landmark in the community.

FIRST BAPTIST CHURCH
500 West Truman Road

1895

Brickmason: William M. Randall, Independence, Missouri

This edifice was built on the site of an earlier church that was destroyed by fire in November 1894. The red-brick structure occupies an important location at the Truman Road jog of Pleasant Street, forming an effective visual closure for Pleasant Street from the south.

SMITH RESIDENCE
1534 East U.S. 24 Highway

ca. 1896

The exterior of this former farmhouse is covered with clapboard and the gables are shingled. The distinguishing feature is the curving L-shaped porch with elaborate spindle frieze and turned posts. The original owner was Mathew H. Smith.

WAGGONER ESTATE OUTBUILDING
313 West Pacific

1899

Builders: William F. Street, Independence, Missouri, and
Christian Yetter, Independence, Missouri

This small outbuilding is part of the residential complex referred to as the Waggoner Estate. The main house, which was greatly altered by William H. Waggoner in 1899, was originally built for John Lewis immediately after he sold his house at 302 West Mill (shown on page 37). The property was bought in 1864 by George Caleb Bingham, a Missouri genre painter. He is reputed to have begun his Civil War painting "Order No. 11" on this property. The early Santa Fe trail ran along the east side of this property; later it went along the west side. The twenty-two-acre site is still intact and seems ideally suited for a park.

1921 Joseph T. Bird Mausoleum   Architect: McDonnell & Sons,
Barre, Vermont

MOUNT WASHINGTON CEMETERY
614 South Brookside

1900

Landscape Architect: George Kessler, Kansas City, Missouri

In 1886-87 Willard E. Winner assembled a 2,400-acre tract of land for the creation of Washington Park, an extensive amusement center of great variety, including a lake and cascade. Part of the park was later converted into the 550-acre Mount Washington Cemetery. The landscape design for the cemetery, incorporating the principle of preserving and enhancing the natural topography, was the work of George Kessler. Kessler, the designer of the Kansas City, Missouri, park and boulevard system, was a disciple of Frederick Law Olmsted, the renowned nineteenth century landscape designer of Central Park in New York City. Among the notable elements of the cemetery are monumental mausoleums and chapels, the enclosing stone wall on Brookside, the north and south entry gates, and the beautiful trees and plantings. The cemetery includes the graves of many prominent area residents, including Jim Bridger, a major figure in the opening of the West.

101

"The choice of beautiful spots for the repose of the dead is one of the surest tokens of a refined and progressive civilization...."
—Kansas City Star, September 26, 1900.

1907 Mrs. John Long Memorial Chapel
Architect: Adriance Van Brunt, Kansas City, Missouri

1909 Henry E. Lantry Mausoleum

1911 Charles Campbell Mausoleum
Architect: Frank Maynard Howe, Kansas City, Missouri

RESIDENCE
304 East Elm

ca. 1900

Builder: Fred E. Siebolt, Independence, Missouri

This clapboard workman's cottage, similar to many other homes built in Independence at the turn of the century, shows great simplicity and strength. It is remarkable because it has remained relatively unchanged.

CRICK RESIDENCE
1210 West Lexington

ca. 1901

Above the first-story facings of this cut-stone and frame residence, the exterior walls are covered with dark green slate shingles. Interesting features include the small projecting gables that occur at the apex of each of the major gables and the three-sided staircase bay.

The original owner was William Crick, founder of the Independence Stove and Foundry Company in 1892.

SMITH RESIDENCE
1214 West Short

ca. 1904

Builder: John D. White, Independence, Missouri

This was the residence of Joseph Smith III, first president of the Reorganized Church of Jesus Christ of Latter Day Saints. Urged by many church members to move to Independence from Lamoni, Iowa, he decided to do so in 1906. Smith selected this house for its unpretentiousness and purchased it from John D. White. It has remained in the Smith family ever since. The original narrow clapboard siding has been covered with asbestos siding.

BENTON SCHOOL
512 East Kansas

1904

Architect: L. Grant Middaugh, Kansas City, Missouri
Builder: Robert L. McBride, Independence, Missouri
Brickmason: William M. Randall, Independence, Missouri

Benton School, demolished by the Independence School District in 1977, was an exemplary turn-of-the-century hipped-roof schoolhouse in the midst of a pleasant and quiet residential area.

Robert L. McBride's father, who settled here in the mid eighteen forties, was one of the earliest known builders in Independence.

William M. Randall came to Independence in the mid eighteen fifties.

STONE ARCH BRIDGE
East Truman Road and Blue Ridge Boulevard

1906

Contractor: Swenson Construction Company,
Kansas City, Missouri

Constructed of native fieldstone, this single arch spans Truman Road at Blue Ridge Boulevard and forms a strong visual gateway to Independence. At this point in the approach to the city from the west, the Reorganized Church of Jesus Christ of Latter Day Saints Auditorium becomes visible as a major landmark.

LUFF RESIDENCE / ART CENTER
1034 West Lexington

ca. 1906

This pleasant brick structure with its unusual square tower has been adapted to house the Independence Community Art Center. Its corner location, coupled with its high visibility, makes it an important landmark along Lexington. The Joseph Luff family occupied the house from 1907 until 1917. Dr. Luff was the first director of the Independence Sanitarium from 1909 to 1912.

KERBY RESIDENCE
9867 East Winner Road

ca. 1906

Builder: Rufus O. Kerby, Kansas City, Missouri
Architect: Rupert O. Kerby, Independence, Missouri

The Kerbys, working as a team, designed and built this house; Rupert Kerby lived in it for a short time. Among the interesting features are the fascinating play of the small gables within the large gable roof, the Doric posts on the first floor supporting Ionic posts above, and the strongly accentuated stone-masonry.

GEORGEN RESIDENCE
933 South Main

ca. 1905

Carpenter: Charles A. Doty, Independence, Missouri
Stonemason: William C. Howard, Kansas City, Missouri

The original owners, John and Adele Georgen, designed this house and supervised its construction. John Georgen was a prominent lawyer in Kansas City, Missouri. Adele Bryant Georgen entertained extensively in this bold, craggy fieldstone residence, which was then surrounded by large lawns.

COREY RESIDENCE
138 West Sea

ca. 1905

The semicircular arched boxed gable is an architectural motif frequently found in Independence residential architecture. Decorative siding and an oriel window at the stair landing are interesting features.

The original owner was George W. Corey, who was deputy county treasurer in 1907.

MOUNT WASHINGTON METHODIST CHURCH
584 South Arlington

1907-08

Architect: John H. Felt and Company, Kansas City, Missouri

In contrast to the many other additions to buildings in the city, the 1927 annex on the church's north by architect Ernest O. Brostrom of Kansas City, Missouri, fits in well with the earlier structure. The church, the Mount Washington School with curving stone retaining wall, and the Mount Washington Masonic Lodge all contribute to the pleasant environment of this area at the intersection of Arlington Street and Independence Avenue.

BARBER SHOP
THOMPSON JEWELRY
SHOE
THOMPSON JEWELRY
JEWELER
RIVIERA SHOP
MODERN SHOE REPAIR
FRED WILLIAMSON
CL 4-5950

STREET BUILDING
208-212 West Lexington

1908

Builder: William F. Street, Independence, Missouri

In 1908 William Street remodeled his building with a new brick facade; it had previously served as the depot for Willard E. Winner's Kansas City, Independence, and Park Railway—the Dummy line—the first streetcar line to Independence. The remodeling included apartments on the second floor. Transoms are hidden under present signs.

Street had been a partner with Christian Yetter on several Independence construction projects, including the 1899 remodeling of the Waggoner estate. He was well known in business, political, and lodge circles and served as a member of the City Council from 1903 to 1905.

123

HAMANN RESIDENCE
415 North Eubank

ca. 1910

Architect and Builder: Louis W. Swan, Independence, Missouri

This house is an example of the shingle-style bungalow that had gained popularity elsewhere in the United States but was rare in Independence. The residence is further distinguished by its arched boxed gables incorporating a Persian curve at the base. The first resident was W. C. Hamann.

NORFLEET RESIDENCE
127 East Kansas

ca. 1910

The original owner, Clyde K. Norfleet, allegedly won the money to build this house by gambling in Kansas City. The house is constructed of random fieldstone with a red tile roof. The tree-trunk porch posts are concrete, cast from molds of trees that grew in the old Benton School yard. The doorbell is wired into a cannonball. The arched fieldstone porch railings are found in several residences in Independence.

CITY HALL
200 South Main

1910

Architect: Robert L. McBride, Independence, Missouri
Contractor: Christian Yetter, Independence, Missouri

The City Hall was erected under the leadership of Mayor Llewellyn Jones. Designed by a local architect and built by a local contractor, this is the only city hall erected for Independence. The structure relates well in scale to the buildings on the Square one block to the north and surpasses most of them in appearance. Although the interior has been badly neglected, the building provides much space that could be converted into useful and attractive facilities.

SWOPE - WATSON FARM RESIDENCE
17500 East Kentucky Road

ca. 1912

"Esperanza," now Cedarcrest Farm, was the country residence of Thomas H. Swope, the nephew of Thomas E. Swope, donor of Kansas City's Swope Park. This suburban estate is graced by magnificent trees that contribute greatly to the setting. A bowling alley in the basement runs the length of the house and pergola behind. Nearby, a wooden entrance gives access to a domed brick springhouse.

The Edward T. Watson family has owned and operated Cedarcrest Farm since 1938.

FIRST CHRISTIAN CHURCH
125 South Pleasant

1919

Architect: John H. Felt and Company, Kansas City, Missouri
Contractor: Christian Yetter and Robert L. McBride, Independence, Missouri

The first church on this site was built in 1908 and was domed. It was partially destroyed by fire in February 1918 and was rebuilt the following year. Under the guidance of the original architect, the remaining walls were incorporated into a similiar structure.

CHURCH OF JESUS CHRIST OF LATTER-DAY SAINTS
302 South Pleasant

1914

Architect: James Oliver Hogg, Kansas City, Missouri
**Builder: M. L. Fogel Construction Company, Kansas City,
Missouri**

This red-brick structure, trimmed with cream-colored terra-cotta, is adorned with cartouches featuring the Star of David and paired tablets. Joseph Fielding Smith, president of the Latter-day Saint church, delivered the dedicatory prayer at services held on November 22, 1914.

INDUSTRIAL BUILDING
600 South Cottage

ca. 1915

Headlined in the local newspaper as a facility to "manufacture substitute for horses on farm," this square fieldstone industrial structure was used to manufacture tractors. The building was sold in 1920 to the Independence Airless Tire Company and was later used as a laundry and cabinet shop. It now serves as a warehouse. The original owner was James E. Hare, merchant and auctioneer.

McCOY RESIDENCE
701 South Park

ca. 1915

Architect: William Stewart McCoy, Independence, Missouri

Designed by McCoy for his wife and himself, this house reflects the influence of Frank Lloyd Wright and his "Prairie School." Mr. McCoy, grandson of the first mayor of Independence, was himself elected mayor in 1920.

Map of the Growth Years

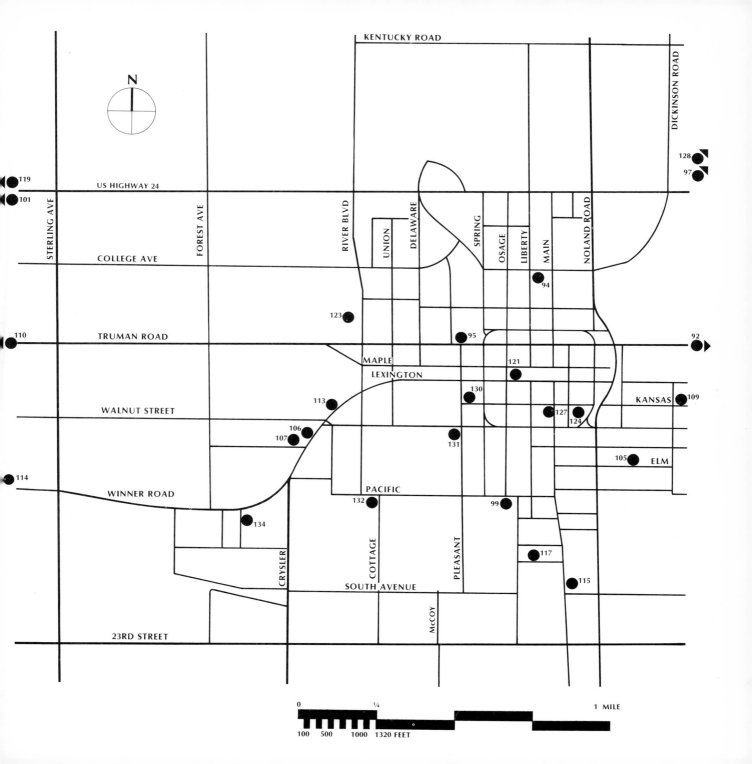

Wars, Depression, and Recovery

The United States entered World War I in April 1917 and mobilized its armed forces. Independence youths in Batteries C and D, and others in Battery F, including Harry Truman—all of the 129th U.S. Army Field Artillery—left for training at Fort Sill, Oklahoma, on September 26, 1917.

In 1918 the 129th landed in France and moved to the front line. Sergeant Vincent Bowles, a local youth killed just before the armistice was signed on November 11, 1918, wrote a friend about a battle in which he and his comrades fought:

A couple of boys from Independence fell that day. Their names will never be forgotten. . . . I will never forget the sights I saw on that field that day. I am proud to be a member of that division, just one of the cogs of the great machine. . . . I am an American, and am glad that I live at this day when our country needs her best men. . . .We are doing it for our mothers, sisters, friends and the coming generation and it is worth any hardships we go through for them.

The veterans who returned from the war went quickly to work. They became the movers of commerce in the city during the nineteen twenties and also began to take over city and county politics. William Stewart McCoy, one of the veterans, was elected mayor of the city in 1920. At the time of his nomination the *Examiner* reported that "the selection of Mr. McCoy was a triumph for the younger element in the party. He had the unanimous support of the ex-servicemen among the delegates. . . ." Another fledgling politician was Harry S. Truman, who was elected in 1922 as eastern judge of the Jackson County Court, an administrative position. Roger T. Sermon, also a World War I veteran, was elected mayor in 1924. He was to be reelected continuously to this position until his death in 1950.

During the nineteen twenties, Independence again prospered. New stores and homes were erected and older ones remodeled. Gleaner-Baldwin—now Allis-Chalmers—began manufacturing combines here in 1925. So many other businesses were also started during those years that even after the crash of the stock market, a report on business in Independence in 1929 stated that "the year just closed was the best in a decade and 1930 will beat it." But Chamber of Commerce optimism proved unrealistic in the face of the growing depression that gripped the nation. In 1931 Mayor Sermon formed a committee of the heads of civic organizations "to give wholehearted support to a definite plan for providing work, whereby those out of employment in Independence may provide for themselves and their families the necessities of life this winter."

The county also arranged work for the unemployed. During this period the courthouse was rebuilt in its present design under the aegis of Presiding Judge Truman. In another project the 1859 jail was renovated as a community welfare office. A free federal-state employment office was located on the first floor and the second floor was used for women's sewing projects. The kitchen was used to teach canning and 92,000 tin cans were stored in the old jail.

On the Federal level, the Works Progress Administration funneled money into Independence making it possible to build a new junior high school and improve Slover Park. Even the sales of several new homes were advertised during the year.

Independence was now over one hundred years away from its pioneer beginnings. A

1939 article in the Independence *Examiner,* entitled "City Losing Its Pioneer Identity," warned:

One by one links with our hardy fore-fathers have been obliterated....Independence is asleep insofar as its pride in the past is concerned....Businessmen in this city should rally around and plan to salvage what few things are left that tell the story of our glorious past when this town was carved out of the wilderness and was the farthest west outpost, when covered wagons streamed out of here. Those were days that the present generation knows nothing about....

To emphasize the city's pioneer heritage, in 1940 Raymond Blake, local newspaperman and historian, conceived the idea of a festival to celebrate the historic trails which left Independence. During the three-day celebration, the Jackson County Historical Society marked early homes. The *Examiner* stated that "fine new homes and pretty modern bungalows will go unnoticed as Independence celebrators of the Santa-Cali-Gon pay respects to old brick buildings, log cabins, shanties and old mansions." The festivities were extremely popular, drawing a crowd estimated between 60,000 and 85,000 to the Square. Newspaper coverage of the events exceeded the coverage of the war in Europe that had commenced in September 1939.

Although Independence was already emerging from the economic chaos of the depression years, the Second World War accelerated the recovery. The United States had begun manufacturing goods for the Allies. Senator Harry S. Truman, elected in 1934, was influential in securing the Lake City Ordnance Plant for this area; its construction was well under way by 1941. After the bombing of Pearl Harbor, the entry of the United States into the war on December 7, 1941, increased the demand for war materiel.

The building of a major defense industry in the fields of eastern Jackson County had a strong effect on nearby Independence. New gas lines were installed and electric power lines were extended. Highways were improved, but increasing traffic in the city became a problem. More policemen were added to the force and a radio broadcasting unit was installed at the police station. To accommodate new residents, housing developments spread throughout the area.

Between 1916 and 1945, Independence gradually changed from a residential suburb and an agricultural center to a business center with suburbs of its own. These new economic patterns, based on better roads and more automobiles, began fragmenting the physical continuity of the old town.

HOLLAND-SERMON RESIDENCE
11425 East Winner Road

1920

The Lou Holland family lived in this house from the nineteen twenties to mid nineteen forties. Holland, considered one of the fathers of aviation in the area, was instrumental in securing the T.W.A. headquarters for Kansas City and was influential in the development of the Kansas City Municipal Airport. William H. Sermon, who was mayor of Independence from 1958 until his resignation in October 1961, also lived in this house.

SALVATION ARMY FRESH AIR CAMP
16200 East U.S. 40 Highway

1924

This free camp, now known as Mo-Kan, was first used as a summer camp by hundreds of needy urban women and children. Frank C. Niles, a Kansas City cigar wholesaler and philanthropist, initiated the project and in 1924 donated the funds for the land and the dining hall. In 1975 the cottages were moved from elsewhere on the site to their present hillside location. In addition to the summer camp, the camp is now used year-round for a variety of educational purposes.

AUTOMOBILE SHOWROOM
10401 East Independence Avenue

ca. 1924

The automobile age brought the development of a new building type—the walk-in showroom and maintenance building. From this building, decorated with fanciful terra-cotta facing and ornament, Claude P. Brown sold and serviced Fords from 1924 to 1932.

GASOLINE AND SERVICE STATION
9301 East Wilson Road

1925

This gas station is an early example of the building type that developed as the automobile became the major means of transportation in the city. Milo E. Tinkham, the first operator, sold Standard Oil products here from 1925 until 1933.

COMMERCIAL BUILDING
11031-11037 East Winner Road

1926

Contractor: Homer Vaughn, Independence, Missouri

Built by Homer Vaughn, promoter and developer of the
Englewood Plaza, this commercial structure is designed in
a tapestry brick style. The intimate scale of the Englewood
Plaza shopping area seems to imply personal service.

WORLD HEADQUARTERS FOR THE
REORGANIZED CHURCH OF JESUS CHRIST OF LATTER DAY SAINTS
1001 West Walnut

1926

Architects: Henry C. Smith, Independence, Missouri;
            and Bloomgarten and Frohwerk, Kansas City, Missouri
Associate Architect: Joseph Martin, St. Louis, Missouri
Contractor: Weeks Construction Company, Kansas City, Missouri

Under the leadership of President Frederick Madison Smith, ground was broken for the Auditorium in 1926. The building, which was expected to be finished in 1930 for the 100th anniversary of the church, was not officially completed until 1962. The original cost estimate in 1928 was $750,000. By 1962 over four million had been spent on the building.

The dominant feature of the building is the 211-foot free-span dome. The 5,800-seat assembly hall has been the setting for many Reorganized Church of Jesus Christ of Latter Day Saints world conferences, as well as countless civic and cultural functions, including numerous concerts on the world-renowned Aeolian Skinner pipe organ. The lower-level dining room hosted the February 5, 1953, homecoming dinner for newly retired President Harry S. Truman.

153

HILL COUNTY PARK
East 23rd between Ralston and Maywood

1927

The Jackson County Court accepted a 12-acre gift in 1927 as a memorial to William M. Hill, son of Adam Hill, 1833 Jackson County pioneer. The Hill family cemetery, located within the park, includes the graves of their relatives, Alexander F. James and his wife, Anne Ralston James, granddaughter of Adam Hill. The park, which now includes 20 acres, features Rock Creek, natural topography, sycamores, and limestone outcroppings.

FIRE STATION NO. 1/CITY OFFICES
219 North Main

1928

Architect: Hal Wheelock, Independence, Missouri
Contractor: J. E. Dunn, Kansas City, Missouri

This fire station, built on the site of an earlier fire station and later used as a community theater, now houses city offices. Although it was built seventy years later, the station was designed to harmonize with the adjoining marshal's house. These two buildings, together with others in the same block, contribute greatly to the historic character still associated with the Square.

FIRE STATION NO. 2/CITY SHOP
1215 West Elm

1928

Architect: Robert L. McBride, Independence, Missouri
Contractor: L. G. Yankee, Independence, Missouri

The old 1908 firehouse has a new facade with wider doors to accommodate wider fire trucks. Originally Fire Station No. 2, it now serves as a sign shop for the city.

CARNES RESIDENCE
616 North Union

1930

This one and one-half story wood frame cottage is distinguished by its interesting interplay of roof lines. The original owner was Edward K. Carnes, well-known newspaperman in Independence.

GASOLINE AND SERVICE STATION
401 West Maple

1930

Contractor: Orville Campbell, Independence, Missouri

This Skelly super-service station, constructed of brick from the William M. Randall residence formerly located on this corner, is faced with white glazed brick and Spanish tile cornices.

GOLDEN ACRES SUBDIVISION
East Gudgell and Manor Road

1931

**Developer: Kroh Brothers Development Company,
        Kansas City, Missouri**

Golden Acres is a subdivision that has retained its desirable environmental characteristics. General use of similar building materials and careful utilization of landscaping elements, including street trees and fieldstone retaining walls, contribute to the high quality of this neighborhood.

COUNTRY CLUB / COMMUNITY CENTER
1717 South Lake Drive

1933

**Architect: Herbert E. Duncan, Sr., Kansas City, Missouri
Builder: Kroh Brothers Development Company,
        Kansas City, Missouri**

Originally built as a one-story potting shed for a nursery, this structure was remodeled and expanded in 1933 to contain an apartment, office, and clubhouse for the Golden Acres golf club. It now serves as a community center for the subdivision. The flat-roofed two-story stucco building was designed in the modern style of the early nineteen thirties.

TRUMAN COURTHOUSE
112 West Lexington

1932-1933

**Architects: Keene and Simpson, Kansas City, Missouri, and
David Frederick Wallace, Kansas City, Missouri
Contractor: Weeks Construction Co., Kansas City, Missouri**

The present building, which was inspired by Independence Hall in Philadelphia, incorporated portions of six earlier Jackson County courthouse structures and additions. Construction of the first courthouse on this site was begun in 1828. During the second Civil War Battle of Independence, the building served as a military headquarters and a hospital. Judge Harry S. Truman held office in the courthouse from 1923 until 1924 and from 1927 until 1934. Judge Truman's office and the courtroom were restored in 1973.

SERMON RESIDENCE
701 Procter Place

1935

Contractor: Orville Campbell, Independence, Missouri

The original owner was Roger T. Sermon, grocer and mayor of Independence from 1924 until his death in 1950. He served during years of much city expansion and development. The house is an example of the fine character of the residential neighborhood near Winner Road.

DODGION STREET POWER PLANT/ COMMUNITY CENTER
North Dodgion and East Truman Road

ca. 1932

Engineer: Black & Veatch, Kansas City, Missouri

In addition to the imposing smokestacks, the dominant external feature of the former municipal power plant is the west facade containing round brick arches. Construction is now under way for the conversion of this building into a community center.

COUNTY HIGHWAY DEPARTMENT OFFICES AND GARAGE
1030 South Crysler

ca. 1938

Architect: Marshall and Brown, Kansas City, Missouri

These buildings, financed and built by the Works Progress Administration for Jackson County, relate well to each other and form an easily identified landmark in the neighborhood. This was the second project of an office that later became a well-known architectural firm in the region. Asphalt now replaces an earlier lawn.

MUNICIPAL BUILDING
200 South Main

ca. 1939

The Works Progress Administration built this stone structure as headquarters for the distribution of relief supplies. Roger T. and William Sermon, brothers and mayors of Independence, also used this structure as headquarters for planning election strategy. The building was demolished in 1976 by the Independence Urban Renewal Authority.

Map of Wars, Depression and Recovery

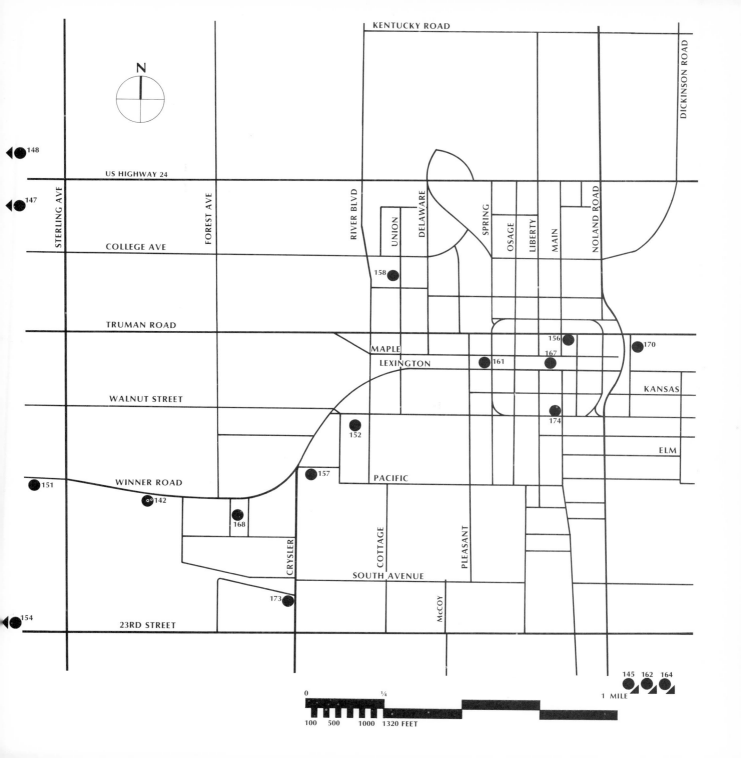

N

KENTUCKY ROAD

DICKINSON ROAD

148

US HIGHWAY 24

STERLING AVE

147

FOREST AVE

RIVER BLVD

UNION

DELAWARE

SPRING

OSAGE

LIBERTY

MAIN

NOLAND ROAD

COLLEGE AVE

158

TRUMAN ROAD

MAPLE

LEXINGTON

156

167

170

161

KANSAS

174

WALNUT STREET

152

ELM

WINNER ROAD

157

PACIFIC

151

142

168

SOUTH COTTAGE

PLEASANT

CRYSLER

SOUTH AVENUE

McCOY

173

154

23RD STREET

0   ¼   1 MILE

100 500 1000 1320 FEET

145 162 164

Expansion Years

"It's a relaxed old town, almost wholly Southern in feeling, where everybody is friends, kinfolks, or feuding....Much of the town, which styles itself 'Queen City of the Trails,' shows the fading splendor of another age...," observed a 1950 *Saturday Evening Post* article about Independence in a series on United States cities.

Independence is still a relaxed old town—friendly, proud of its heritage from the trail days—but Independence is also different now, no longer resembling a small Southern town. In 1950 Independence's population was 37,000; in 1966 it had reached 100,000; and by 1976 Independence was the fourth largest city in Missouri with 120,000 inhabitants.

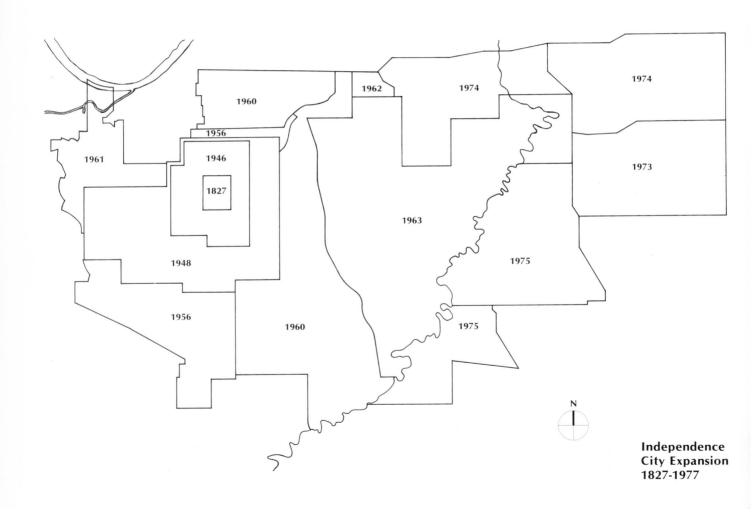

**Independence
City Expansion
1827-1977**

In January 1948 Independence had the same boundaries as in 1889, but on the twenty-seventh day of that month the citizens voted to annex areas on all sides of the city, enlarging it from 3.4 to 10.3 square miles and nearly doubling the population. Determined to retain the growth potential for Independence in the face of an expanding Kansas City, Mayor Roger T. Sermon remarked: "I feel that a great future lies ahead of us, and sincerely hope and expect the good will of all citizens of the new area."

More annexations occurred in 1956, 1960, 1961, 1962, 1963, 1974, and 1975, bringing the total area of the city to 78 square miles. New housing developments spread over land formerly devoted to farming as the suburbs grew because of the ever increasing reliance on automobiles. Indicative of this growth are the 20 shopping centers that now serve the Independence area. The newest—Independence Center, a multimillion-dollar regional complex—was built in 1974 in the southeast corner of the city.

As a result of all this suburban activity, retail business on the Square declined. In an effort to revitalize the district, Urban Renewal attempted to improve the flow of traffic and provided landscaping and additional parking. The full impact of this extra effort has yet to be felt, but after more than 150 years, the Square still remains the symbolic as well as the financial and legal center of the community and the county.

MOTOR COURT
1631 Salisbury

1946-1950

Builder: Ray Holder and Sons, Ray Dean and Richard
Duane Holder, Independence, Missouri

Typical cottages of the nineteen twenties and thirties served as examples for this group of simple, repetitive structures.

ENGLEWOOD THEATER
10917 East Winner Road

1949

Architect: Luther Orville Willis, Kansas City, Missouri
Contractor: Homer Vaughn, Independence, Missouri

This post-World War II structure has characteristics of a nineteen thirties modern building, particularly noticeable in the curved wall of the cashier's booth. The building, developed by Homer Vaughn and Virgil Julian, Sr., has stucco exterior walls trimmed with maroon tile wainscoting and edged in limestone.

MESSIAH LUTHERAN CHURCH
613 South Main

1958

Architect: William Fullerton, Kansas City, Missouri
Contractor: Allen Chambers, Kansas City, Missouri

The low, gabled roof and solid vertical masses of brick utilized in the design are typical of modern functional church architecture. A unique feature of the church is a choir room in the 60-foot bell tower.

188

RESTHAVEN NURSING HOME
1500 West Truman Road

1950

Architect: Dane D. Morgan and Associates, Burlington, Iowa
Contractors: Messina Brothers Construction Company, Kansas City, Missouri, and
Weeks and Maxwell Construction Company, Independence, Missouri

The siting and institutional design of this brick building reflect architectural design prevalent in the nineteen fifties. The landscaping and the space formed by the building wings contribute to the pleasant atmosphere of the site. Resthaven was built by the Reorganized Church of Jesus Christ of Latter Day Saints as a home for the elderly.

LATTER-DAY SAINTS MISSION HOME
517 West Walnut

1961

Supervising Architect: Harold W. Burgon,
Salt Lake City, Utah
Contractor: David E. Ross Construction Company,
Independence, Missouri

This contemporary brick ranch-style structure with low-pitched gable roof is well adapted to its sloping site. The landscaping of the hillside reinforces the total design effect.

MEDICAL OFFICE BUILDING
2116 South Sterling

1964

Architect and Contractor: Marshall Erdman,
Madison, Wisconsin

This building of the early nineteen sixties emphasizes its horizontality through brickwork, flat roof lines, banded windows, and low planters. It was built specifically for Doctors Harry S. Jonas and Wallace R. Stacey, obstetricians.

SCHONDELMEYER ANIMAL HOSPITAL
1102 East 23rd Street

1974

Architect: Collaborative Phase One Plus,
Kansas City, Missouri
Contractor: Zebarth-Sanders, Kansas City, Missouri

This sharp-angled building is a good example of the architecture of the early nineteen seventies. The site contains landscaping that relates well to the design of the structure and the boldness of the forms.

TOWNHOUSES
1008-1016 West Maple

1975

Architect: Lund and Balderson, Overland Park, Kansas
Builder: Waldemar Kurok, Independence, Missouri

The attached row housing is well adapted to its sloping site. The natural beauty of the ravine below has wisely been left undisturbed. The horizontal siding is reminiscent of the clapboard siding on earlier nearby residences.

INDEPENDENCE CENTER SHOPPING MALL
I-70 and M-291 North

1974

Architect: Architectonics, Inc., Dallas, Texas
Developer: Homart Development Company,
                Chicago, Illinois
Builder: C. H. Leavell and Company, Chicago, Illinois

This regional shopping center is an example of a large enclosed shopping mall. Particularly noteworthy is the quantity and quality of the public non-rent-producing space. Special attention has been given to providing the shoppers with a variety of spatial experiences.

Map of Expansion Years

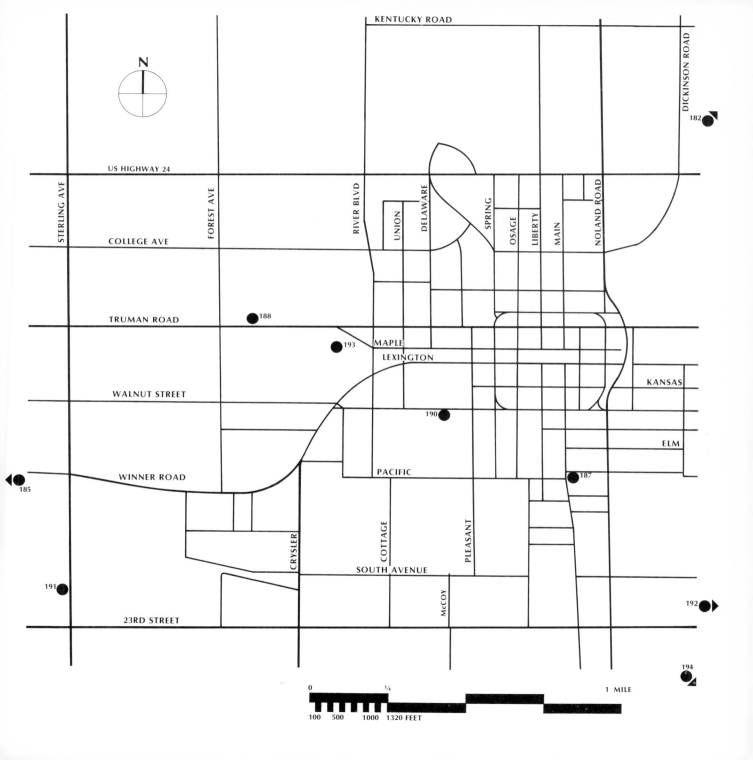

N

KENTUCKY ROAD

DICKINSON ROAD

182

US HIGHWAY 24

STERLING AVE

FOREST AVE

RIVER BLVD

UNION

DELAWARE

SPRING

OSAGE

LIBERTY

MAIN

NOLAND ROAD

COLLEGE AVE

TRUMAN ROAD

188

193

MAPLE

LEXINGTON

WALNUT STREET

KANSAS

190

ELM

WINNER ROAD

PACIFIC

187

185

CRYSLER

COTTAGE

PLEASANT

191

SOUTH AVENUE

McCOY

192

23RD STREET

194

0   ¼   1 MILE

100   500   1000   1320 FEET

The Truman Heritage

"Independence is the best place in the world." With these words, Harry S. Truman indicated the depth of his love for his hometown, a feeling and a place to which he referred again and again:

Mr. Truman was fond of saying that to him Independence was what Hannibal, Missouri, was to Mark Twain. He liked to quote what Twain said late in his life in a speech in India, "All the *me* in me is in a little Missouri village halfway around the world."

The Truman family moved to Independence in 1890, when Harry was six years old; he grew up here during one of the finest periods in its history. His cousin, Miss Ethel Noland, has commented on the civilized atmosphere of that time: "There was conversation. I mean by that talk about what was going on in the world, talk about ideas." Judge Albert A. Ridge of the United States District Court in Kansas City and veteran of Battery D remarked, "When Harry was a boy, it seems to me that there was more a sense of moral value than there is now, more a sense of community life."

Harry Truman said of his youth: "I had just the happiest childhood that could ever be imagined." He was sent to Sunday school at the First Presbyterian Church, where he first met Bess Wallace. About this event he later recalled, "I was too backward to look at her very much and I didn't speak to her for five years." From the fifth grade on he attended grammar school with her; they were graduated from high school together and their entire courtship took place in and around Independence. They were married in 1919 in Trinity Episcopal Church on North Liberty Street and made their permanent home in the Wallace family residence at 219 North Delaware Street.

In 1922 Harry Truman was elected eastern judge of Jackson County. Daughter Mary Margaret was born in the Delaware Street house in 1924. Truman served as United States Senator from Missouri from 1934 until he was elected Vice-President in 1944. Then, on April 12, 1945, Harry S. Truman became President of the United States when Franklin Delano Roosevelt died.

Harry Truman voted for himself in the Memorial Building on Maple Avenue in 1948. While visiting his home on Delaware Street in 1950, Truman learned of the invasion of South Korea. In 1953, after he turned over the responsibilities of the presidency to General Dwight David Eisenhower, Harry S. Truman returned by train to his beloved Independence.

The Kansas City *Star* reported that a crowd of approximately 8,500 persons assembled to greet him at the Missouri Pacific Station on his arrival:

"Thank you very much," Mr. Truman said humbly, a slight choke appearing in his voice. "I can't tell you how much we appreciate this reception. It's magnificent—much more than we anticipated. It's a good feeling to be back home."

In Independence, memories of Harry Truman linger in the minds of relatives, friends, army comrades, fellow politicians, neighbors, and acquaintances. But memories fade and someday all who know him will be gone. We can, however, preserve some of the city that shaped him. We can keep what remains of buildings, sidewalks, and landscapes he cared about for those who come after us. The Harry S. Truman Library and the Harry S. Truman Historic District, an officially designated National Landmark, give hope for the survival of some of the Independence he lived in and loved.

TRUMAN HOME
219 North Delaware

1885

Architect and Builder: James M. Adams,
Independence, Missouri

This was the home of Mr. and Mrs. Harry S. Truman from the time of their marriage in 1919 and the Summer White House during Truman's Presidency. The section shown here was added in 1885 to a house built in 1867 for George Porterfield Gates of the Waggoner-Gates Milling Company. His daughter, Margaret, married David Willock Wallace. Elizabeth (Bess) Wallace Truman is their daughter. The original roof was of hexagonal slate.

TRINITY EPISCOPAL CHURCH
409 North Liberty

1881

Architects: Sturgis and Brigham, Boston, Massachusetts
Carpenter: James M. Adams, Independence, Missouri
Brickmason: William M. Randall, Independence, Missouri

This church is purported to be the only example of a John Sturgis-designed structure west of the Allegheny mountains. Sturgis is credited with introducing Victorian Gothic, of which this church is an example, in America.

Bess Wallace and Harry S. Truman were married here on June 28, 1919; their daughter Margaret married Clifton Daniel here in 1956.

NOLAND - HAUKENBERRY RESIDENCE
216 North Delaware

ca. 1886

Originally built for A. T. Slack, local merchant and grocer, this house incorporates a structure dating back to the eighteen fifties. In 1908 Margaret and Joseph Tilford Noland, aunt and uncle of Harry S. Truman, bought this house. As a young man, Truman visited here often, particularly while courting Bess Wallace, who lived across the street. He sometimes stayed all night with the Nolands after a late date rather than returning to the family farm in Grandview.

REESE RESIDENCE
903 West Waldo

ca. 1885

This building, demolished in 1977, was first occupied by Nathan Reese, a farmer. It originally was a mirror image of that at 909 West Waldo, which has since been extensively remodeled. The latter house was purchased by Mr. and Mrs. John Truman in 1895, and their son, Harry S. Truman, spent his teen years there.

FIRST PRESBYTERIAN CHURCH
100 North Pleasant

1888

Architect: Nier, Hogg and Byram, Kansas City, Missouri
Contractor: Christian Yetter, Independence, Missouri

This red-brick church is visually dominated by three elaborate rose windows, each centered in a gable. The bell tower is capped by an octagonal spire and the sanctuary is laid out in a modified Akron plan. In recent years, the building has been carefully preserved and restored.

Harry S. Truman attended Sunday school and met Bess Wallace here in 1892. Some sixty years later he reminisced, "The other morning, I passed the Presbyterian Church at Lexington and Pleasant, where I went to Sunday school. I remember a golden-haired girl. She's still golden haired to me [pointing to Mrs. Truman]."

GENTRY RESIDENCE
722 West Waldo

ca. 1890

Distinguished by its curving porch with spindle frieze and turned posts, this house, moved here from another site, retains much of its original character. It is currently occupied by Miss Sue Gentry and her brother, Harvey Gentry. Miss Gentry's friendship with the Trumans and her long career as a newswoman in Independence have made the house especially well known in recent years.

MISSOURI PACIFIC RAILROAD STATION
600 South Grand

1913

Harry S. Truman arrived and departed from this depot during his Presidency and his whistle-stop campaign of 1948. The brick passenger platforms used by Mr. Truman were removed in 1971 when all passenger service to this station ceased. The original roof was Spanish tile.

MEMORIAL BUILDING
416 West Maple

1925-1926

Architect: Alonzo Gentry, Independence, Missouri
Contractor: M. T. Colgan, Independence, Missouri

Now occupied by the Parks and Recreation Department, this cross-shaped building was built for the City of Independence as a memorial to those who lost their lives in World War I. It was also used as headquarters for and activities of various civic organizations. Harry S. Truman held his only Independence press conference in this building and voted for himself here in 1948.

Harry S Truman on a morning walk

Independence was the home of a famous pedestrian. President Harry S Truman cherished his walks along the streets of his hometown. Much of contemporary life has become dependent on the use of automobiles and several newer streets are inhospitable to walkers. Energy shortages and the need for physical exercise may cause us to rediscover the values of walking or bicycling in safe, attractive, and friendly neighborhoods.

Map of Truman Heritage

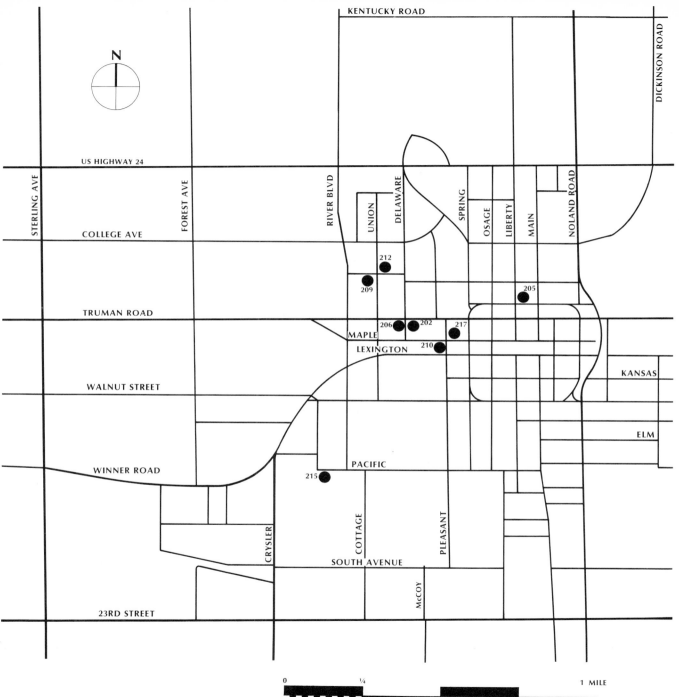

Future Directions

In retrospect it is possible to understand the sequence of past events, but predictions tend to be less accurate than historic analyses. While many forces that will affect preservation in Independence can be identified, many developments could emerge from present conditions. Much will depend on leadership within the community, on public understanding of the issues, and on the quantity and quality of citizen participation in the decision-making process.

It is no easy task to assimilate large numbers of new citizens into a city that wishes to retain its historic identity and small-town friendliness. The Heritage Commission hopes that the publication of this book will lead to thoughtful discussions and effective actions to enhance and preserve what is best in Independence. There already are indications of a growing local awareness of historic and environmental values.

Appreciation of heritage can lead to civic responsibility. As a nation and as individuals, we benefit from the wise actions of those who went before us; we also owe a debt to the future. The greatest threat to Independence would be a citizenry that stopped seeing or caring. Civic consciousness must include an awareness of the environment.

From among several promising areas in the city, the Heritage Commission has chosen the Truman Historic District as the site for its first attempt to encourage private and public effort at neighborhood revitalization. The commission also plans to develop and to seek support for such programs in other areas of the city.

Many old structures in Independence are well kept. In some instances where maintenance has been inadequate, buildings have benefited from lack of improvements so that original exteriors and details have been retained. Some other buildings that have undergone unfortunate although often expensive alterations can still be readily restored. Individual owners and occupants of buildings that need to be repaired are encouraged to do so. In any neighborhood, repair can be just as catching as neglect.

Nobody is required to read books, listen to music, go to the theater, or visit museums, but we spend most of our lives in surroundings made by people. This makes environmental design an unavoidable art. Today many individuals spend a large part of their waking hours in surroundings that provide little beauty, refreshment, or delight. Too often we don't even notice the quality of our visual experiences, but in closing our minds to the trashiness of much of our scene we also deprive ourselves of considerable pleasure. To start looking again will bring about enchantment and anger; it will take both of these emotions to improve our environment.

This book is published at a critical time. Since the Second World War, homogenizing influences have grown stronger everywhere in our country. Mobility has loosened the ties between individuals and their community. Technological skills have overcome the demands of climate and terrain and permitted the construction of buildings inappropriate to their location. Loss of distinctiveness has diminished our enjoyment of places.

All across the country we are beginning to realize again that individual buildings do not exist in isolation and that aside from their intrinsic values, many elements in our surroundings are significant because of their relation to the larger setting. We have found that *newer* does not automatically mean *better*. We are learning that repair and adaptation to changing needs are often less costly than demolition and new construction. We have discovered that highways do not have to destroy the urban fabric. We now know that massive urban surgery can be very disruptive and occasionally fatal. We have begun to see that economic considerations and limited resources make disposable environments unreasonable and that consideration of human needs makes them undesirable.

Preservation in Independence could have remained an antiquarian movement of charm and irrelevance. Valuable as it is in itself, the enshrining of a few isolated places of historic or architectural significance has no major effect on daily living. Only through the integration of many physical elements from the past into our ordinary experiences will we sense the continuity of human existence. It is to the great credit of the Heritage Commission that it has recognized preservation as an environmental act.

Among the elements that help make Independence unique are the visible evidences of its history: the terrain, the structures of architectural quality, the railroads, the springs and streams, the trees and plants, the neighborhoods and the historic districts. These elements will have to be crucial considerations in the private and governmental decisions that will determine the future development and character of Independence.

Environments worth saving means history worth remembering, joys worth reliving, civilization worth preserving. Healthy conservation efforts today play a significant part in preparing for tomorrow.

Summary Maps

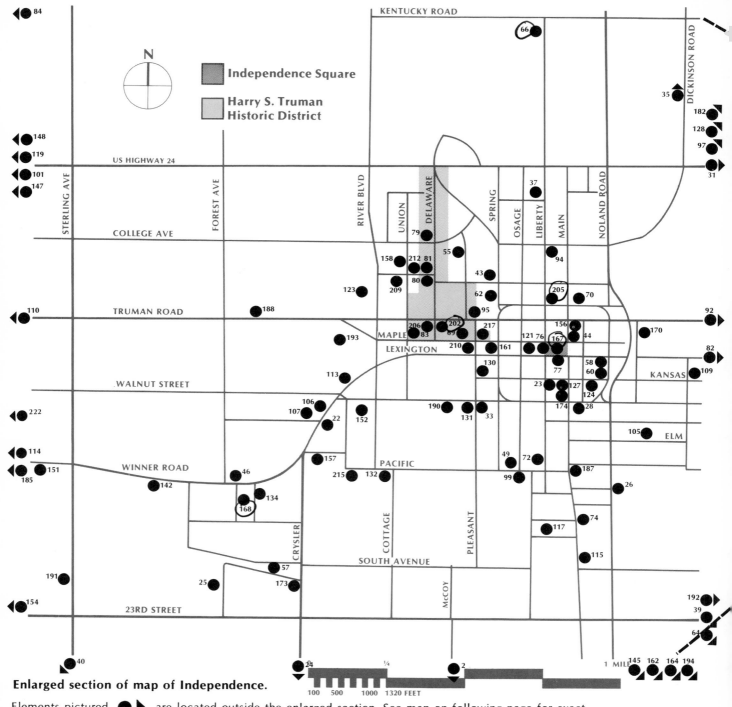

Enlarged section of map of Independence.

Elements pictured ⬤▶ are located outside the enlarged section. See map on following page for exact location.

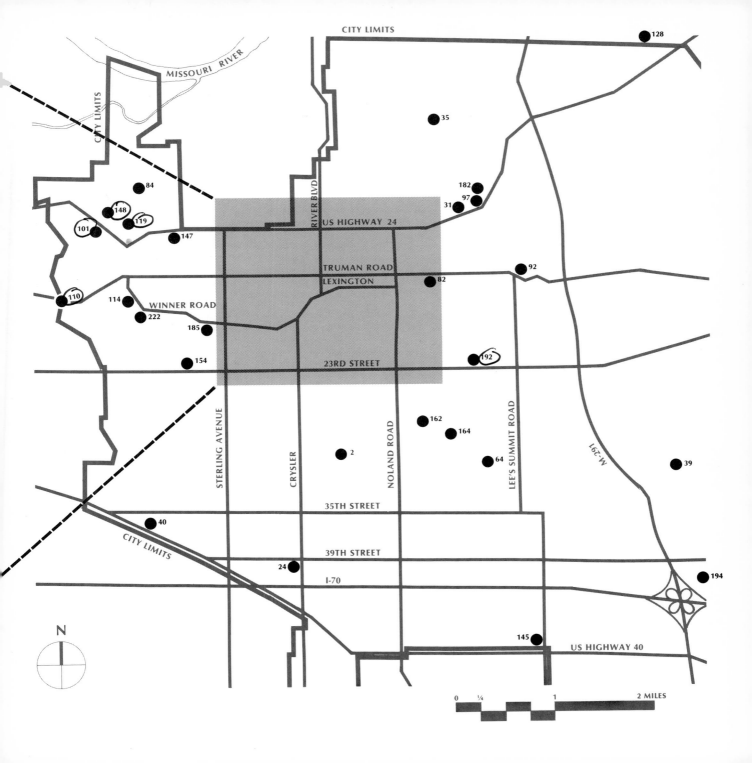

MISSOURI RIVER

CITY LIMITS

CITY LIMITS

●128

●35

RIVER BLVD

182
●

31 97
● ●

US HIGHWAY 24

●84

148
119

101
●

147
●

TRUMAN ROAD

●92

LEXINGTON

●82

110

114
●

WINNER ROAD

222
●

185
●

154
●

23RD STREET

192

STERLING AVENUE

CRYSLER

NOLAND ROAD

162
●

164
●

LEE'S SUMMIT ROAD

M-291

●2

●64

●39

35TH STREET

●40

39TH STREET

CITY LIMITS

24
●

I-70

●194

145
●

US HIGHWAY 40

N

0   ¼   1   2 MILES

List of 431 Survey Elements

The following list contains the 431 elements surveyed under contract for the Heritage Commission of the City of Independence. Other sites and structures will be added later.

*Mount Washington Methodist Church
*584 South Arlington

Residence
621 South Arlington

Residence
625 South Arlington

Residence
1600 South Arlington

Residence
1607 South Arlington

Residence
1610 South Arlington

Bridge
900 Block South Ash

Fairmount Christian Church
641 South Ash

Residence
1533 South Ash

Cemetery
1901 Blue Ridge Boulevard

Residence
3854 Blue Ridge Boulevard

Residence
3884 Blue Ridge Boulevard

Residence
120 Bowen Court

Residence
122 Bowen Court

Residence
1227 North Broadway

Residence
210 North Brookside Avenue

Residence
511 South Brookside Avenue

*Mount Washington Cemetery
*614 South Brookside Avenue

Farmhouse
Bundschu between Powell and Bly Road

Residence
903 South Cedar

Residence
1121 South Claremont

Bryant School
827 West College Avenue

Bungalow grouping
1301-1401 West College Avenue

Residence/Antique Shop
1403 West College Avenue

*Industrial Building
*600 South Cottage

Gas Station/Commercial Building
Intersection South Crysler and West Lexington

*County Highway Department Offices and Garage
*1030 South Crysler

Residence
4207 South Crysler

Residence
3839 South Crysler

*Henley-Williamson Residence
3940 South Crysler

Residence
4207 South Crysler

*Noland-Haukenberry Residence
216 North Delaware

*Truman Home
219 North Delaware

Residence
304 North Delaware

Residence
310 North Delaware

Residence
318 North Delaware

Residence
403 North Delaware

Residence
411 North Delaware

Residence
423 North Delaware

Residence
426 North Delaware

*Sawyer-Jennings Residence
510 North Delaware

Residence
511 North Delaware

*Fletcher-Bostian Residence
602 North Delaware

Burr Oak Tree
610 North Delaware

Residence
627 North Delaware

*Bullene-Choplin Residence
702 North Delaware

*Cemetery
Opposite 921 Dickinson Road

Residence
1536 Dickinson Road

Log Cabin and Pioneer Spring
North Dodgion and East Truman Road

*Power Plant/Community Center
North Dodgion and East Truman Road

231

---

*Indicates survey elements pictured.

*Residence
304 East Elm

Residence
1201 West Elm

*Fire Station No. 2/City Shop
1215 West Elm

*Hamann Residence
415 North Eubank

Mount Washington School
570 South Evanston

Residence
1539 South Evanston

Residence
1610 South Evanston

Residence
1700 South Evanston

Lake
Fairview and Lake Drive

Double House
115 East Farmer

*McCoy Residence
410 West Farmer

*Noland-White Residence
1024 South Forest

Residence
708 South Fuller

*Missouri Pacific Railroad Station
600 South Grand Avenue

Residence
418 North Grand Avenue

*Golden Acres Subdivision
East Gudgell and Manor Road

Residence
516 South Hardy

Residence
1 Hawthorne Place

Residence
2 Hawthorne Place

Church
610 North High

Residence
820 North Home Avenue

Residence
1016 South Home Avenue

Residence
534 South Huttig

Residence
9500 East Independence Avenue

Residence
9504 East Independence Avenue

Masonic Lodge
9515 East Independence Avenue

Commercial Building/Apartment
9605 East Independence Avenue

Mount Washington Baptist
Church
9623 East Independence Avenue

Commercial Building
10106 East Independence Avenue

Commercial Building
10205-10209 East Independence
Avenue

Commercial Building
10229 East Independence Avenue

Commercial Building
10305 East Independence Avenue

*Automobile Showroom
10401 East Independence Avenue

*Independence Center Shopping
Mall
I-70 and M-291 North

Cottonwood Tree
Jones between River Boulevard
and McCoy

Residence and Barn
1008 North Jones

*Norfleet Residence
127 East Kansas

Residence
131 East Kansas

Residence
132 East Kansas

Residence
136 East Kansas

Residence
141 East Kansas

*Pohlmeyer Residence
146 East Kansas

*Benton School
512 East Kansas

*Log Courthouse
107 West Kansas

Commercial Building
123 West Kansas

Residence
9701 East Kentucky Road

*Swope-Watson Residence
17500 East Kentucky Road

232

Residence
18315 East Kentucky Road

Farmhouse
Lake City Valley Road south of
East U.S. 24 Highway

Farmhouse
Lake City Valley Road at Carswell
Road

Farmhouse
Lake City Valley Road south of
Carswell Road

*Country Club/Community Center
1717 South Lake Drive

Residence
2525 Lee's Summit Road

Glendale Farm
2909 Lee's Summit Road

*Drumm Farm
3210 Lee's Summit Road

Adair Park
4111 Lee's Summit Road

Residence
825 South Leslie

Bridges
West Lexington and South Crysler

Commercial Building
107 East Lexington

Commercial Building
121-129 East Lexington

Commercial Building
109-113 East Lexington

Commercial Building
139 East Lexington

Commercial Building
141-143 East Lexington

*Rummel Residence
147 East Lexington

St. Paul A.M.E. Church
200 East Lexington

Warehouse/Commercial Building
301 East Lexington

*Wilson-Colyer Residence
602 East Lexington

Temple Site Marker and Church
of Christ-Temple Lot Church
†West Lexington and South River
Boulevard

*Truman Courthouse
†112 West Lexington

Commercial Building
115 West Lexington

Commercial Building
119 West Lexington

Commercial Building
121-123 West Lexington

*Street Building
208-212 West Lexington

Choplin Building
209-211 West Lexington

Slover's Drive-In
921 West Lexington

RLDS Stone Church
1012 West Lexington

*Luff Residence/Art Center
1034 West Lexington

Residence
1038-1040 West Lexington

Commercial Building/Apartments
1106 West Lexington

*Crick Residence
1210 West Lexington

Smith Study
1233 West Lexington

*Flournoy House
1233 West Lexington

Residence
1305 West Lexington

Commercial Building/Apartment
1327-1337 West Lexington

Commercial Building/Apartments
1401-1411 West Lexington

Commercial Building
1415-1425 West Lexington

Gasoline Station/Commercial
Building
1420 West Lexington

Residence
1600 West Lexington

*Woodson Residence
1604 West Lexington

*Bank/Commercial Building
200 North Liberty

Watkins Building
205 North Liberty

Commercial Building
202-206 North Liberty

*Trinity Episcopal Church
409 North Liberty

*St. Mary's Roman Catholic Church
611 North Liberty

Residence
801 North Liberty

Residence
815 North Liberty

Residence
1124 North Liberty

*Vaile Mansion
†1500 North Liberty

233

Parking Structure
Northeast corner South Liberty
and West Kansas

*Staples Residence
526 South Liberty

Residence
619 South Liberty

Residence
623 South Liberty

Residence
1321 West Linden

Procter School
1403 West Linden

Commercial Building
101 North Main

Bundschu Building/City Hall
103 North Main

Commercial Building
111 North Main

Commercial Building
203 North Main

Commercial Building
207-209 North Main

Commercial Building
208-212 North Main

Commercial Building
215 North Main

***Marshal's House and County
Jail/Museum**
†217 North Main

*Fire Station No. 1/City Offices
219 North Main

Residence
424 North Main

Church
500 North Main

Residence
714 North Main

Residence
718 North Main

Residence
802 North Main

Residence
825 North Main

Residence
1222 North Main

Jones-Erwin Residence
1400 North Main

Carl Building
101-103½ South Main

Commercial Building
109 South Main

Commercial Building
119 South Main

Commercial Building/Eagles Lodge
124 South Main

*City Hall
200 South Main

*Municipal Building
200 South Main

Bridge
300 Block of South Main

Commercial Building
316-318 South Main

Residence
519 South Main

*Messiah Lutheran Church
613 South Main

Residence
619 South Main

Residence
722 South Main

Residence
725 South Main

Residence
728 South Main

*Hughes-Gregg Residence
801 South Main

Residence
907 South Main

Residence
910 South Main

Residence
915 South Main

*Georgen Residence
933 South Main

Residence
1004 South Main

Residence
1106 South Main

Residence
1216 South Main

Residence
1220 South Main

Commercial Building
120 East Maple Avenue

234

†Listed on the National Register of Historic
Places

Commercial Building
125 East Maple Avenue

Commercial Building
100 West Maple Avenue

Commercial Building
106-108 West Maple Avenue

Commercial Building
202-204 West Maple Avenue

Commercial Building
209 West Maple Avenue

Commercial Building
211 West Maple Avenue

Commercial Building
213 West Maple Avenue

Commercial Building
224-230 West Maple Avenue

Commercial Building
308 West Maple Avenue

*****Gasoline and Service Station**
401 West Maple Avenue

Commercial Building
411 West Maple Avenue

*****Memorial Building**
416 West Maple Avenue

Gasoline Station/Commercial Building
423 West Maple Avenue

*****Porter-Chiles Residence**
522 West Maple Avenue

Residence
601 West Maple Avenue

Residence
611 West Maple Avenue

Watson-Eberle Residence
720 West Maple Avenue

William Chrisman Junior High School
709 West Maple Avenue

Residence
801 West Maple Avenue

Residence
803 West Maple Avenue

Residence
814 West Maple Avenue

Residence
815 West Maple Avenue

Residence
905 West Maple Avenue

Apartment Building
908 West Maple Avenue

Residence/Apartment Building
911 West Maple Avenue

*****Temple Place Town Homes**
1008-1016 West Maple Avenue

Central Police Building
223 North Memorial Drive

*****Lewis Webb Residence**
302 West Mill

Farmhouse
17200 R. D. Mize Road

Farmhouse
17601 R. D. Mize Road

*****Summer Kitchen and Farmhouse**
18525 R. D. Mize Road

*****Woodlawn Cemetery**
701 South Noland Road

Residence
800 South Noland Road

Residence
1000 South Noland Road

Residence
1114 South Noland Road

Residence
1301 South Noland Road

Residence
1325 South Noland Road

Bristol School
1500 South Northern Boulevard

Residence
1734 South Northern Boulevard

Residence
1916 South Norton

Commercial Building
214 North Osage

Vaile Mansion Carriage House
*1518 North Osage

Residence
218 South Osage

Residence
509 South Osage

Residence
518 South Osage

*****Waggoner-Gates Mill**
526 South Osage

Industrial Building
1618 South Osage

*****Mifflin Residence**
108 South Overton

Carriage House/Residence
114 East Pacific

Residence
123 East Pacific

Residence
126 East Pacific

Residence
127 East Pacific

Residence
143 East Pacific

*Waggoner Estate
313 West Pacific

Residence
629 South Park

Residence
641 South Park

*McCoy Residence
701 South Park

Catalpa Tree
826 South Park

Residence
1400 East Parker

Residence
109 South Pendleton

Residence
116 South Pendleton

Residence
202 South Pendleton

Residence
206 South Pendleton

Residence
213 South Pendleton

Residence
217 South Pendleton

*First Presbyterian Church
100 North Pleasant

Residence/Commercial Building
101 North Pleasant

Jackson Residence
300 North Pleasant

Residence
406 North Pleasant

Residence
407 North Pleasant

Residence
409 North Pleasant

Residence
415 North Pleasant

Residence
424 North Pleasant

Residence
501 North Pleasant

Residence
513 North Pleasant

Residence
514 North Pleasant

Residence
518 North Pleasant

Mercer-Wilcox Residence
116 South Pleasant

*First Christian Church
125 South Pleasant

*LDS Church
302 South Pleasant

†Overfelt-Johnston Residence
305 South Pleasant

Dodd-Williamson Residence
313 South Pleasant

Residence
1014 South Pleasant

Residence
637 Procter Place

Residence
638 Procter Place

Residence
640 Procter Place

Residence
700 Procter Place

*Sermon Residence
701 Procter Place

Residence
702 Procter Place

Residence
720 Procter Place

Residence
724 Procter Place

Residence
725 Procter Place

Residence
1440 South Ralston Avenue

Residence
403 North River Boulevard

Residence
512 North River Boulevard

Residence
602 North River Boulevard

Residence
726 North River Boulevard

Mound Grove Cemetery
1818 North River Boulevard

Residence
414 South River Boulevard

Residence
420 South River Boulevard

Residence
426 South River Boulevard

Street, Houses, Cemetery Wall
100 Block of East Ruby

Residence
120 East Ruby

Residence
109 West Ruby

Residence
117 West Ruby

Residence
129 West Ruby

Residence
200 West Ruby

Residence
206 West Ruby

Residence
105 East St. Charles

*Motor Court
1631 Salisbury Road

Residence
18000 Salisbury Road

Santa Fe Trail Ruts
Opposite 3122 Santa Fe Road

Residence
119 West Sea

*Corey Residence
138 West Sea

Residence
338 West Sea

Residence
426 West Sea

Residence
208 East Short

*Smith Residence
1214 West Short

Residence
1400 West Short

Residence
1503 West Short

Residence
1601 West Short

Residence
1611 West Short

Apartment Building
1623-1629 West Short

Residence
702 East South Avenue

Residence
411 West South Avenue

Residence
524 West South Avenue

*Chicago and Alton Railroad Station
1411 West South Avenue

Residence
314 North Spring

Residence
322 North Spring

Residence
404 North Spring

*McCoy-DeWitt Residence
412 North Spring

Fire Station No. 1
950 North Spring

Waggoner-Gates Mill Office/ Tavern
570 South Spring

Residence
1801 South Sterling

Residence
1804 South Sterling

Residence
1808 South Sterling

Residence
1830 South Sterling

Residence
1855 South Sterling

Residence
1900 South Sterling

*Medical Office Building
2116 South Sterling

Residence/RLDS Church
2121 South Sterling

Residence
2651 South Sterling

*Stone Arch Bridge
East Truman and Blue Ridge Boulevard

Webb Castle
9015 East Truman Road

Commercial Building
9601-9605 East Truman Road

Residence
10201 East Truman Road

Gasoline Station
10401 East Truman Road

Residence/Day Care Center
10736 East Truman Road

Residence
15211 East Truman Road

*__Brookside Farm__
16000 East Truman Road

*__First Baptist Church__
500 West Truman Road

Residence/Apartment Building
800 West Truman Road

*__Resthaven Nursing Home__
1500 West Truman Road

Hospital/Medical Office Building
1509 West Truman Road

Residence
401 North Union

*__Carnes Residence__
616 North Union

Residence
701 North Union

Residence
702 North Union

Residence
710 North Union

Residence
117 South Union

Residence
121 South Union

Residence
123 South Union

Residence
127 South Union

Truman Library and Grave Site
East U.S. 24 Highway at Delaware

Motor Court
711 East U.S. 24 Highway

*__Springhouse__
1300 East U.S. 24 Highway

*__Smith Residence__
1534 East U.S. 24 Highway

*__Thomson Residence/Restaurant__
9800 East 40 Highway

*__Salvation Army Fresh Air Camp__
16200 East U.S. 40 Highway

Residence
711 West Waldo Avenue

Residence
718 West Waldo Avenue

*__Gentry Residence__
722 West Waldo Avenue

Residence
810 West Waldo Avenue

Residence
820 West Waldo Avenue

*__Reese Residence__
903 West Waldo Avenue

Truman Boyhood Home
909 West Waldo Avenue

Residence
1105 West Waldo Avenue

Residence
1115 West Waldo Avenue

Residence
1123 West Waldo Avenue

Blake Museum
103 East Walnut

*__Kritser Residence__
115 East Walnut

*__LDS Mission Home__
517 West Walnut

Court of Residences
518-522 West Walnut and 218
South Pleasant

*__RLDS Auditorium__
1001 West Walnut

Residence/Apartment Building
1110 West Walnut

Residence
914 South Washington

**Road, Rock Creek and Rock Creek
School**
South Hardy and Westport Road

Burr Oak Tree
Harris and Westport Road

*__Second Baptist Church__
116 East White Oak

Residence
816 West White Oak

Residence
900 West White Oak

Residence ·
1315 West White Oak

Residence
1433 South Willow

Residence
1439 South Willow

*__Gasoline and Service Station__
9301 East Wilson Road

*__Fairland Heights Bus Station__
9900 Block East Winner Road

Bridge
East Winner Road at Home

Residence
9518 East Winner Road

Residence
9535 East Winner Road

Residence
9717 East Winner Road

Residence
9725 East Winner Road

Residence
9755 East Winner Road

Residence
9835 East Winner Road

Residence
9836 East Winner Road

*Kerby Residence**
9867 East Winner Road

Residence
9875 East Winner Road

Residence
9883 East Winner Road

Residences/Graceland College
9900 East Winner Road

Commercial Building
10815 East Winner Road

*Englewood Theater**
10917 East Winner Road

Commercial Building
11026 East Winner Road

*Commercial Building**
11031-11037 East Winner Road

Residence
11312 East Winner Road

Residence
11328 East Winner Road

*Holland-Sermon Residence**
11425 East Winner Road

Residence
11426 East Winner Road

Residence
11500 East Winner Road

Residence
11501 East Winner Road

Residence
11514 East Winner Road

Residence
11521 East Winner Road

Residence
11601 East Winner Road

Commercial Building
11701 East Winner Road

Residence
11607 East 9th Street

Residence
10211 East 10th Street

Residence
10425 East 15th Street

Residence
9715 East 16th Street

Residence
10500 East 18th Street

Residence
11501 East 19th Street

Residence
10902 East 20th Street

*Hill Park**
East 23rd Between Ralston and
 Maywood

*Schondelmeyer Animal Hospital**
1102 East 23rd Street

Coil's Grocery
900 West 23rd Street

Residence
1104-1106 West 23rd Street

*Santa Fe Trail Ruts/Santa Fe Trail
 Park**
West 29th and Santa Fe Road

Residence
10100 East 31st Street

Residence
12810 East 39th Street

Selected Sources

The complete notes and exact references for quotations and information contained in this book are available in the files of the Heritage Commission at Independence City Hall. For further study into Independence history, the commission recommends the following sources:

Franzwa, Gregory M., *The Oregon Trail Revisited,* Patrice Press, St. Louis, 1973.

Hickman, W. Z., *History of Jackson County, Missouri,* Historical Publishing Co., Topeka and Cleveland, 1920.

History of Jackson County, Missouri, Union Historical Publishing Co., Kansas City, 1881.

History of the Reorganized Church of Jesus Christ of Latter Day Saints, 8 Vols., Lamoni and Independence, 1896-1976.

Journal, the Jackson County Historical Society, Independence, 1959 to date.

Miller, Merle, *Plain Speaking,* Berkeley Publishing Co., 1973.

Poppino, Hattie E., Abstractor of U.S. Federal Census of 1830, 1840, 1850, and 1860 for Jackson County, Missouri, 1959, 1964.

Rice, Martin, *Rural Rhymes & Talks and Tales of Olden Times,* Hudson-Kimberly Publishing Co., Kansas City, 1893.

Slavens, J. W. L., *Illustrated Historical Atlas of Jackson County, Missouri,* Brink-McDonough and Co., Philadelphia, 1877; Reprint, Jackson County Historical Society, 1976.

The Independence Examiner, Independence, 1905 to date, and Centennial Edition, September 30, 1927.

Truman, Harry S., *The Truman Memoirs: Year of Decisions* and *Years of Trial and Hope,* Doubleday, Inc., 1955 and 1956.

Truman, Margaret, *Harry S. Truman,* William Morrow and Co., New York, 1973.

Wilcox, Pearl, *Jackson County Pioneers,* Independence, 1975.